From
Mare + Bethan
Christmas 1996.

W. L. Davies
Srem-y-Maes.
Bewlah
New Castle Emlyn.

REFLECTIONS
of a Country Vet

Eric I. Williams

Professor Emeritus
Oklahoma State University
College of Veterinary Medicine

First Impression—October 1996

ISBN 1 85902 486 6

© Copyright 1996: Dr. Eric I. Williams

First published in January 1996 by New Forums Press Inc.
Oklahoma, U.S.A.

Printed in Wales at
Gomer Press, Llandysul, Ceredigion

Contents

Preface

Fifty-five years ago, I left home in the snow to embark on my professional career. Here I am today, looking out at the snow but thousands of miles away and retired.

After I had been in practice in my home town in Wales for over a decade, I started to jot down some notes on a few of the most interesting episodes in my daily—and nightly—life. I found myself chuckling a lot and vowed to publish them. However, my life changed drastically when my family and I left for Oklahoma, U.S.A. Though fully intent on completing my project, in addition to my college duties I became the editor of *The Oklahoma Veterinarian* and shortly afterwards, *The Bovine Practitioner* for the newly established American Association of Bovine Practitioners.

I continued to write some chapters periodically but it was my retirement in 1988 that really gave me the impetus to finish my project—and here it is!

In the first part of the book, I have traced my life growing up on a dairy farm in a wonderful Christian home, the solid grounding in the 3R's at the elementary school, the superb teachers at the grammar school, the school uniform and how my hero influenced my desire to become a vet.

My college career is recalled, emphasizing the effects of the war (World War II) on our daily lives and the need for a massive increase in food production which brought a totally new image for the veterinary profession as a vital link in this endeavour.

In the chapter entitled 'The Golden Era,' I present a synopsis of my life in a country practice during what my colleagues and I maintain was the most exciting era of veterinary medicine and which has been so superbly portrayed by our esteemed colleague, the late Dr. James Alfred Wight (James Herriot) in his best-selling novels.

In the remaining chapters, I take you with me on my rounds which reflect the joys and sorrows so often encountered. As I look back, I am impressed by that wonderful bond of trust that existed between my colleagues and me and our clients. A successful vet needs to possess a love of people as well as animals.

Most of the time I was accompanied by a veterinary student 'seeing practice' to gain clinical experience as a vital part of graduation requirements. Our conversations as we made our rounds are presented in many instances.

It was this contact with students over the years that eventually led to my momentous decision to accept a teaching position at the Oklahoma State University College of Veterinary Medicine.

I wish to express my sincere thanks to many people, far too numerous to record, who have contributed so much to my interesting life.

Above all, my sincere thanks and love to my wife, Mary and our children, Thomas, Michael and Betsi for their loyal support and encouragement along the way to a life successful far beyond our wildest dream.

January 18, 1996   Eric I. Williams

The Grove Boys

My father was convinced that I would become an auctioneer because I jabbered so much, and mother had aspirations for me to 'enter the Cloth,' but having gone through the fantasy of being a clown in a circus (maybe I am!), ever since I was shoulder high to a Welsh pony, I wanted to be a veterinary surgeon.

I was born on October 13, 1922 (which was also a Friday!). I grew up in a delightful Christian home on a farm known as 'The Grove' near St. Clears, in South West Wales. Dad took over the 180-acre farm when grandfather died in the late 1800s and proceeded to purchase some more land and remodelled the home where my sisters, brothers and I grew up. Dad was an outstanding farmer and the pioneer breeder of Friesian cattle from Holland during the 1910 decade—much to the disgust of his neighbours, who bred Dairy Shorthorn Cattle. His vision paid off in that the herd became one of the best in the nation. Though he had little formal education, Dad was an exceptionally well-informed individual in local and national affairs. He served on local and county councils for many years and on the Board of Governors of Whitland Grammar School, without any financial remuneration. He was a devout Christian who gave many years of service to his chapel as music director, treasurer and deacon. His blueprint for a successful life has been an inspiration to all of us, namely: strive to be the best you can possibly be in your chosen business or profession; accept and implement your civic responsibilities and attend and support your church. He was truly an outstanding farmer, the epitome of a practising Christian and statesman. He implanted in us the essential difference between a statesman and a politician.

Mother was a beautiful lady with flaming red hair. She had a melodious soprano voice and won many competitions in local *Eisteddfodau*. Mam was a wonderful gardener with a great love of flowers. She believed that one is nearest God's heart in a bed of beautiful flowers. Dad had three daughters from his first wife, but she died very young, leaving him with three young children, Ceinwen, Eluned and Megan. He had the tragic experience of losing his second wife soon after the birth of another daughter, Lilwen. Dad and my mother had five boys—four of us closely grouped in age, namely, Dyfrig, Awstin, Iorwerth and Eric (that's me!). I was the fourth, and it took six years for brother Huw to arrive! We were known as the Grove boys, growing up during the 1920s and the Depression of the '30s.

Needless to say, four young sprats were always up to some mischief, though there was usually plenty of work on the farm to keep us occupied. Somehow, one or more of us fell in the mud, tore our trousers climbing trees or were caught fighting. Dad was a stern disciplinarian but never laid his hand (or his cane that he used regularly) on us. One look from him was enough, and if we were in real trouble, we were ushered off to bed without supper—now *that* was real punishment!—but one of our dear sisters would invariably sneak something for us to eat.

It was a real Red Letter Day for me, now a spritely five-year-old, when I arrived for the first time with my brothers to start school. Mother had brought us in the trap and pony to celebrate the occasion. Let me take you along with us on our two-mile journey from our home up five hills to Llanginning (now Llangynin) Council School—and only two hills on the way home. Our farm was on the bottom boundary of the parish, and as we climbed up the hill from the farm

Grove Farm—the farm buildings are below the lower left of this photo.

we went along for a short distance where the road went by the parish church, known as Llangynin Parish Church, which dates from the 14th Century.

We continued past the church for a few yards on to the road leading north where we were usually joined by three others from a neighbouring farm. There was no time to dawdle in the morning because we had to get to school—classes started promptly at 9:00 a.m., so let's go from the school homewards, when we did our visiting. Leaving our two-room school on the hill we would walk past Derlwyn Farm—a small-holding adjacent to the school. None of us liked old Mrs. Harries because when we kicked our football into her garden during playtime she would keep it—or at least until we all went over to beg for its return! Across the road from the farmhouse was the postman's shanty or shed. He would deliver the mail on his bicycle all along the way from the Post Office in St. Clears, three miles away, arriving usually early in the afternoon. The shed was equipped with a small stove where he prepared his lunch, rested and then cycled home. We loved to call on him to hear his stories and some local gossip which he collected on his postal route.

Next we passed Bryn Baptist Chapel in the village centre. The village had only one side street which we nicknamed 'Sodom Street'—I still don't know why, but all the families in the five houses were related! At the entrance to the street there was the cobbler's shop, run by the Lewis family. Halfway down the hill lived old William the tailor—a sprightly, square-shouldered, bald little man who wore a measuring tape over his shoulders and his eye-glasses on the end of his nose. He always came to the farm when Dad needed new suits to take measurements and bring all the local gossip plus his own home-spun philosophy. A few yards down the road was Blaenpant Farm owned by old Jonah Thomas, who was a *real* character—short, stocky, partially bald, with a curling moustache, his neck collar usually a flaming red and white handkerchief, his cap worn sideways. Jonah would lean against the farmyard gate and loved to expound about the ills of society, locally and beyond. His one great objective every year was to be the first to mow hay early in June—and he would get anxious when we used to tease him that our servants had the mowing

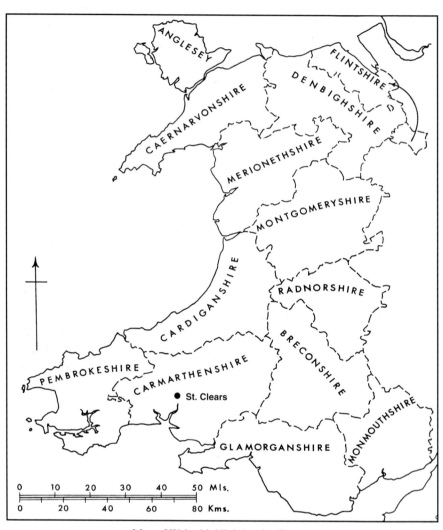

Map of Wales highlighting St. Clears.

machine ready to go! He had an Irish wolfhound named Fly which he really worshipped—and always claimed was the most obedient dog in the parish. One evening one of us decided to test him by asking him to throw his weatherworn cap over the hedge to see if Fly would retrieve it. The old boy duly threw it and called on Fly to show his mettle. To his chagrin, the old dog refused and ran to the house! We were all highly amused but quickly ran away because we wouldn't dare laugh at him.

Continuing our homeward journey, we would drop in on Idris, the local carpenter with a wonderful tenor voice. We marvelled at his skill in building all sorts of farm equipment—gates, ladders, wagons, haysheds and the occasional coffin. He was true to his craft—measure twice and cut once. He was a very meticulous man who took great care of his tools. If any of us got out of line and played with some of them, invariably a quiet command would bring out Bruce, his golden retriever, who would growl at us; and we got the message, especially when he threatened to put us in a coffin!

Our next port-of-call was the local blacksmith, Jim Thomas (*Jim y Gof* or Jim the Blacksmith) who had spent his younger days shoeing pit ponies. We always respected the law of the Smithy, which was enforced when he was shoeing a horse: no messing around! We would fight for turns to blow the bellows to keep the fire alive for preparing the horseshoes. Whenever we did not keep in line, Jim would quietly slip an iron rod into the fire, and when it was red hot, would hold it up as a warning! We really learned a lot from Jim's 'academy'—such as the importance of rhythm in working (the bellows), the proper use of tools as he built the horseshoes from a straight rod, and the importance of timing in the use of hammers. It paid us to keep on the right side of Jim because, when he was not too busy, he made 'hoops' for us. He would take a spare piece of iron rod and mould it into a circle about eighteen inches in diameter, and a long handle with an open hook at the end of it which we used to guide the hoop. It was the 'in' thing at that time, and we often challenged each other to a hooping contest— who could wheel the hoop the fastest over 100 yards or so!

Well, we had only gone about half a mile from school, and next we came to Llain Farm—a small dairy farm run by Willie Davies, who also had a lorry for collecting milk (in churns) from the neighbouring farms and taking them to the milk factory at St. Clears, about three miles down the road. It was at his farm that I first saw a threshing machine in action driven by a steam engine. Threshing day was quite an event in those days. After the morning milking was done, the steam engine whistle was blown which echoed throughout the valley, calling neighbouring farmers to come and help. It was a wonderful sight to see them all gathered and working together so well. I was fascinated by the sound of the thresher and the golden beauty of the grain filling the sacks. When the job was done, they were entertained by the farmer's wife and her helpers to a home-cooked country feast. I must admit, however, that the event sometimes got out of hand—some farmers brewed their own beer which, to say the least, led to 'mystic euphoria,' or to use the local term for too much to drink—'he became three sheets to the wind!' It was nevertheless a golden era of neighbour helping neighbour. This was really brought home to me one evening in the next farm we passed on our way home. It was obvious to us that a very strong burning smell was coming from the hayshed. We even remarked about it to our parents when we arrived home, and in a couple of hours there came a desperate call for help—the hay was

A general view of Llangynin Parish with Grove Farm in the foreground, Llangynin Church, centre, and Llangynin village, top left.
(*Photo by Dr. Robert B. Kamm, Stillwater.*)

on fire due to internal combustion, which can happen when it is not properly harvested. Here again the neighbours worked hard to quell the flames with buckets of water—there were no fire-engines in those days. The next day when we passed on our way to school we were shocked to see the total destruction of the shed and a mound of burnt hay.

Invariably on our way home we would meet old John Day, the roadman. Now, here was another real character—tall, lanky, always wearing a flannel shirt, corduroy trousers and heavy boots (or galoshes in very wet weather). He would lean on his shovel and expound at length on any current topic. John was employed by the District Council to take care of a 'length,' as it was called, a length being a stretch of roadway about 2-3 miles long. His job was to trim the hedgerows, keep the ditches clear for water to flow and trim the roadside so that the grass edges did not encroach on to the road. Once in a while the roads needed resurfacing. Loads of stones were brought to various points, then the stone cutters would come along and break them into gravel. Eventually the road crew would spray tar, which would then be covered by the gravel. The final stage was for the steam roller to come along to finish the job. I was terrified of this machine, to the amusement and derision of my brothers and the other boys! They literally carried me past this menacing monster!

Speaking of fright, we were periodically encountered by a menacing farm dog. We learned very early to hold our ground, because nothing would stir a barking dog more than for us to run away. It was a different story with a neighbourhood bull. One farmer always let his bull run with the cow herd. I recall one particular evening when we were ambling along, watching the birds, picking the occasional wild flower, nuts or blackberries, when a thundering bellowing and snorting were heard from the other side of the hedge— the nasty old bull was coming after us. Now this was a situation to run—we broke the four-minute mile running away from the bull long before Roger Bannister did it officially!

There were some sad occasions when we would meet a funeral procession led by a horse-drawn hearse with glass sides. The driver

Wendy, our favourite dog, enjoys the music with us on our new gramophone (1930).

was always attired in a frock coat and wore a black bowler hat whilst we stood in line on the side of the road and removed our caps.

Once in a while we would come across a family of gypsies encamped along the roadway. These nomadic people were supposedly of Bohemian origin, and dressed accordingly. The family usually consisted of the parents and several children, a mean-looking dog and a couple of ponies to pull their covered wagon. The ponies were invariably piebalds (black and white) or skewbalds (white and another colour, not black). While they were encamped in the neighbourhood they would go round the farms selling their wares, including carpets, kitchen equipment and wood carvings. Each autumn we would look forward to the arrival of *Shoni Winwns*—Johnny the Onions Man. He was one of a group of farmers who came over from Brittany, France to sell onions. The onions were attached to a length of rope hanging from a rod which he carried over his shoulders as he visited the farmers and private houses. We invariably came across one of them on our homeward journey. Johnny spoke the Breton language which is similar to Welsh and we had a lot of fun conversing with him in our native languages—and making sense most of the time!

Eventually we would arrive home, mostly in good time because we did not stop at all the above places every time. When it rained heavily, we had the luxury of one of the servants or my mother coming to fetch us in the trap and pony, and we rode home in style. I should add that in our parish we had a saying, 'If it is not raining, it is going to!'

Now, let's go back to school!

The Governor's trap, with Nancy in harness, on a shopping trip to St. Clears.

The Three R's

Llangynin Board School, later renamed Llangynin Primary School, was a two-room building erected in 1891 of solid stone walls and a slate roof. The two rooms were named *Ysgol Fach* and *Ysgol Fawr*. I started, along with about 15 boys and girls about my age, in *Ysgol Fach*. Our teacher was Miss Lily Lewis, who cycled from St. Clears every day. She was a strict disciplinarian but nevertheless a very compassionate lady. On very wet days Miss Lewis would inspect the children for wet shoes and stockings and proceed to provide dry ones from her cupboard. She also made cocoa drink for our noon meal of sandwiches, which we brought with us— but my parents insisted that there would be no pop (soft drinks) for the Grove boys! I still don't like cocoa!

As the months went by it was time to proceed beyond playing with crayons and clay. Miss Lewis would call us, one by one, to stand at her desk. She would give me a pencil to hold properly and then, placing her hand over mine, teach me to write. This exercise continued daily

Llangynin School.

until she was satisfied that I could venture on my own. There were also reading sessions—all in the Welsh language, which was our native tongue.

Soon we entered a new enterprise—arithmetic! How well do I still recall reciting with the rest of the class:

> Twice one are two
> Twice two are four
> Twice three are six
> Twice four are eight
> Twice five are ten

and so on until we had learned all our tables up to 12. We also learned to write them on our slates and later on lined paper with pen and ink. Oh, how she would scold us if we had blots of ink on our paper! If only I had had a modern biro, or ballpoint pen, it would have saved me several raps across the knuckles!

I was now ready, at the age of eight, to move along with my classmates to *Ysgol Fawr*—a long room where the younger pupils were seated in one half, and the seniors in the other half. Here Mr. Morgan Thomas, the Headmaster, taught us, assisted by a very pretty farmer's daughter named Het Howells. Now it was time to learn another language—English! We were thoroughly drilled in English and Welsh grammar, writing sentences and eventually paragraphs, reading novels and learning poetry, and a lot of arithmetic. There was strict discipline in the classroom. Those who did not comply invariably were caned a couple of strokes across the hand. I was told it hurt! The 'birch' was still in use but only for the very bad boys. One time a 'tough guy' decided to transfer to our school, bragging that he could whip anybody who would put up his fists. One day he was caught by the Headmaster hitting a small boy. He was ceremoniously marched to the boys' cloakroom where, with his trousers dropped, he received three strokes across his bottom. He never came back to our school!

When I became eleven years old, it was time to take the dreaded 11+ examination. This was a comprehensive test in arithmetic and a choice of mainly English or mainly Welsh grammar and composition writing. Several students opted to remain in school until they were 15, and then left to work on farms or local industries. There was no way to graduate to the higher level school without passing this big test. My Dad made it clear to me that if I did not pass I would be coming home to the farm. Miss Lewis had always told me to stick with it, and that I had great things in front of me. Well, after months of drilling in school and heaps of homework, well supervised by my parents, our D-day arrived. It was a beautiful day in late spring. Mam gave me the traditional 'three-penny bit' for good luck, and Headmaster Thomas drove five of us to a neighbouring school where we joined many others for the day-long examination. On our way to the village, a black cat crossed our path—we were very happy, because that was a sure sign of good luck. The worst part was the long suspense waiting for the results, which eventually came two months later. I passed. What a relief!

I left that wonderful two-room school on the hill at the end of the spring term. In retrospect I feel that I was blessed with superb teachers whom we respected then and even more so now. Discipline in and out of class and a solid grounding in the Three R's were truly the

Headmaster Morgan Thomas with his pupils in *Ysgol Fawr*.
The author is on the front row, left and his brother Huw third from the right
in the second row.

Awstin, Dyfrig, Iorwerth, and Eric with the farm servants Arthur, Tom, and Beecher. (1934)

Feeding the pet lambs.

In the hayfield.

Bethlehem Congregational Chapel; Note the "big pew" in front and under the pulpit,
where the deacons sat.

foundation for an academic future. It was not all R's all the time! On St. David's Day (which I shall refer to later) we sang songs in honour of St. David, our Patron Saint, and the girls dressed in native costumes. Good Friday was a national holiday. All the neighbourhood gathered for the annual tea followed by a concert by the school children who always had a hot-cross bun to take home.

Before Christmas, our friend, Jim the Blacksmith, was the perennial Father Christmas (Santa Claus) who brought us oranges, apples and a small gift.

The Three R's provided a solid base to build my academic career and there was another R—namely, Respect, which was so well taught at home, the Chapel and School.

The Grove family

Aim High

It was now the summer of 1934, right in the middle of the Depression. Times were hard, and Dad only received six pence a gallon for milk. A good dairy cow fetched about ten pounds. Even so, life on the farm was reasonably good. What we never had we never missed. We did not have a car, and there were no tractors, no electricity or a telephone. The postman arrived every weekday at 8:30 a.m., having walked from the local village, and brought the daily newspaper. There were plenty of milk, eggs, meat, and vegetables. Dad kept us busy with farm chores most of the time, but we did manage to play cricket, soccer— and a lot of fighting! As I reflect on those days, even though we fought a lot, throughout the ensuing years my brothers and I have never quarrelled.

Mother spent a lot of time in her flower garden and marshalled our help to do the weeding, mow the lawns, and gather fruit. During a 'good' summer we had lots of delicious red apples, plums and pears. One day my brother Awstin and I had a competition to see who could eat the most apples. When we had devoured about 15 apiece we called it quits. We were both as sick as dogs and received a spanking! Even though we hated picking gooseberries, blackberries, and raspberries, we loved the tarts that my mother and sisters prepared—with lots of fresh cream!

Collecting eggs and cleaning the chicken coops were regular chores. There were times when some chicks or old hens needed burial. That was a special occasion when we held mock funerals, covered the grave with wild flowers, and sang a farewell hymn—accompanied by the farm dogs who howled either in sympathy or because of our poor singing!

This was the summer when Dad bought the first car for the family—one of the first in the neighbourhood. My sisters, Lilwen and Megan learned to drive and chauffeured Dad to his various meetings and all of us to Bethlehem Congregational Chapel, about three miles away, for morning and evening services and afternoon Sunday School—but only on very wet days! Other times we still had to walk

Pendine Sands: during the author's youth there were very few cars and the beach was
a real haven for a picnic, swimming, and playing games.

across the fields, along the railway and up the road to the chapel. The
real treat was to motor to the seaside at Pendine, about nine miles
from home. Pendine has a long beach, where the tide on the ebb goes
out about half a mile, leaving a long stretch of sand for us to build
castles or play soccer or cricket. When the tide was far out we would
race to the sea and have lots of fun splashing and chasing each other.
Then we would race back, ready for a picnic my mother had prepared.
It was from this beach in 1933 that Jim and Amy Mollison took off in
their two-engine plane to attempt a trans-Atlantic crossing. They were
given a rousing send-off by a large crowd of well-wishers. They got as
far as Newfoundland. Pendine sands were the scene of many an
attempt to break the land speed record by famous racing stars,
including Sir Malcolm Campbell and Parry Thomas. A visit to the
beach was never complete without the treat of ice cream in the form of
a tuppenny cornet (two-penny cone), chips wrapped in newspaper
(with plenty of vinegar), and on the way home, a stop in Laugharne
for a bucketful of cockles. When we arrived home we would fill the
bucket with water and listen to the shells pop open. Cockles made
quite a feast.

It was now the beginning of September 1934 and I was getting ready for the next big step in my life—joining my brothers at Whitland Grammar School. The town of Whitland is about five miles west of our home. It was the home of Hywel Dda who was the great lawgiver of Wales in the Middle Ages. In 930 A.D. he proclaimed himself as the King of Wales, summoned leading clergy and representatives from all over the country to Whitland and gave them forty days to propose a unified and codified system of law.

Along with my brothers and all the other pupils, I had to wear a school uniform. It consisted of a grey shirt, a navy blue blazer with the school emblem on the breast pocket, short grey trousers, knee-length grey stockings, red and blue striped tie and a navy blue cap also carrying the school emblem. On each emblem was the school motto: *I fyny fo'r nod*—(Aim High). Failure to be properly attired in the school dress called for disciplinary measures. It was also our custom to 'touch our cap' when we were greeted by someone. The girls wore sleeveless navy blue tunics over long sleeved white blouses. Full-length black stockings were also required. A school uniform is undoubtedly the answer to every mother's dream!

To get to school we walked across a couple of fields, then along a parish road for about half a mile to the main road, where we were picked up by the school bus and on to Whitland. I started along with about 30 classmates in the first level, known as Form Two. (I still have not found Form One or why there was none!) We sat two to a desk, with the boys on the right half and the girls on the left of the classroom. Classes started at 9:00 a.m., and we left school at 3:45 p.m. Throughout the four years, we studied the following subjects:

> English language and literature
> Welsh language and literature
> French language
> History—mainly British, European and some American
> Geography—the whole world!
> Arithmetic
> Geometry
> Algebra

General Science—elementary biology, chemistry
and physics
Woodwork   *(I dropped these two subjects in the*
Music   *final year to concentrate on science.)*

Two double periods a week were devoted to physical education, mainly in the gymnasium and partly on the soccer or cricket field for boys, and field-hockey, net-ball and rounders for the girls. No sporting events or extrac-urricular activities were held during school hours, except that the soccer, cricket, and hockey team players were excused from the final afternoon period whenever they entertained visiting teams or played away games. Here again there was a high standard of discipline. Failure to do our homework, fighting, or misbehaviour in the classroom resulted in being given detention—usually one extra hour of classwork at the end of the day. Sometimes the Headmaster would use his prerogative to use the cane. There was *never* any doubt that the teachers were totally in charge of the school with the support of the Board of Governors and the parents.

As for our teachers, they were the very best. They wore academic gowns in the classroom. We had nicknames for all of them; starting with the Headmaster, Mr. D. S. Richards—we called him *Oiseau*, which is French for bird. He was a stern man with a distinct Roman nose and a very good physics teacher. Mr. James Mathias—Matthew—taught history in a superb manner. He really made great events come alive. We learned all the important dates from 1066 to The Great War (1914-1918). He was tall with flowing black hair. He was the father of William Mathias, the distinguished composer. Mr. E. C. Davies was our geography teacher—we called him *Dai Bach* because he was short and stocky with flashy blue eyes and bushy eyebrows. He also taught physical education to the boys (the girls had a different visiting teacher). Mr. Davies taught us well. Among many other things we knew every major river, mountain, ocean, capital citiy, etc., in the world. Because of his short build, once in a while some of the school bullies would needle him for a fight. They regretted it, for *Dai Bach* was a polished boxer.

Mr. Tom Rees, *Tombey*, taught French. Our Welsh teacher was

Mr. James Llewelyn—we called him *Llew* or *Garibaldi*, since he was a rotund, bald person. He was also a very good producer of plays.

Miss G. M. Evans taught geometry, algebra, and biology. She was *Ginger* because of her beautiful hair. She was an exceptionally good writer on the blackboard. Mr. Frank Goddard went by the name of *Jouey*. He taught chemistry. An Englishman, he was a great teacher but a tough disciplinarian who sometimes would reveal his bad temper. Miss Jones, *Tubby*, was a short, rotund woman who taught music and cookery. Mr. Austin Thomas, the woodwork class teacher, was quite a character. We called him *Austin Bai* because he always said 'bai' instead of 'boy'. He was short, partially bald with a mop of grey curls overhanging his ears. Sometimes he would get confused, to our amusement, when he would say, 'Listen to the (black) board and look at me!' He was a master craftsman who took great care of his tools—and woe to anyone who abused them.

Undoubtedly the Queen of the classroom was Miss E. A. Roberts— Miss Bobs. She was a tall, impressive lady with straight black hair and a prominent bosom. She was our English teacher, loved and dreaded by all her pupils. Before her class period we would sneak down the corridor to enquire from the other pupils, 'How is old *Bobs* today?' If they said 'Look out, she is in her bad mood' we all cringed with fear. She demanded extra effort from her pupils and came down heavily on pupils who butchered the English language; she taught English grammar 'with a vengeance'. In our literature classes we learned reams of poetry which were assigned to us as homework. The next day she would randomly call on individuals to stand and recite the assigned homework. If the pupil had not learned the poem she would unload her wrath on him or her—and sometimes boxed our ears, which certainly got our attention! I now admit that, in spite of the terror she often created in our hearts, she was a great teacher and beyond the school walls a very charming, dignified lady. I am glad now that she made me learn all that poetry and lots from 'Julius Caesar'. My favourites are:

'I wandered lonely as a cloud
That floats on high o'er vales and hills
When all at once I saw a crowd
A host of golden daffodils;
Beside the lake, beneath the trees,
Fluttering and dancing in the breeze.'
                    Wordsworth's *I wandered lonely as a cloud.*

'There is a tide in the affairs of men
Which, taken at the flood, leads on to fortune.'
                    Shakespeare's *Julius Caesar*

'And slowly answered Arthur from the barge
The old order changeth, yielding place to new
And God fulfills himself in many ways
Lest one good custom should corrupt the world.'
                    Tennyson's *Morte d'Arthur*

'Friends, Romans, countrymen,
Lend me your ears.
I come to bury Caesar, not to praise him.
The evil that men do lives after them
The good is oft interred with their bones.'
                    Shakespeare's *Julius Caesar*

Whenever former pupils get together, the conversation always turns towards Auntie Caro. This delightful lady ran a shop across the street from school, where we bought sweets, chocolates, pop and miscellaneous items. To some of the boys it was a source of cigarettes, their favourite being 'tuppenny' (2 pence) Woodbines, 5 to a pack. During play-time they would sneak into her backyard for a whiff.

Our school year was divided into three terms, starting in September and ending early July, with Christmas and Easter holidays in between. Assigned homework received a letter grade on the scale of A, A-, B+, B, B-, C+, C, C-. At the end of each term there were three-hour examinations called terminals in each subject. In most subjects, we had the choice of six essay questions out of eight. Each test was graded out of 100, with 50+ being a passing grade. However, it was usually hard to achieve! There were *never* any true/false or multiple choice questions (not even at the College level).

I had aspirations to become a veterinary surgeon at an early age. My Uncle Tom was a successful farmer who also was quite knowledgeable on farm animal diseases. Dad usually called him whenever he had a sick animal. I enjoyed watching and helping him. Uncle was now getting old and could only handle minor cases. Mr. Roger Thomas, the local vet, lived in Carmarthen, about ten miles away. Nothing seemed to bother him. When he did come to treat an animal he would then stay for lunch or tea.

In the early 1930s things began to change. Mr. Thomas was joined by a young graduate named Mr. A. T. Morgan, known as Bob. He was tall, handsome, as strong as a bull and drove his Rover car around the farms at lightning speed (or so it seemed), to the delight and envy of the local farm boys. He was the heart-throb of all the girls! One Sunday morning, he came to the farm to attend to old Naomi (every cow had a name) with a prolapsed uterus. Bob took care of it with ease and then the servants brought a ewe which was having difficulty lambing. Bob sorted out her problem—twin lambs with one presented normally, the other coming backwards (hind legs first). He delivered the lambs much to their mother's relief and our joy.

Now I really wanted to be like my new hero, so one Saturday morning I jumped on the bicycle which I shared with my brothers, dressed in my school uniform with my cap at the usual angle and journeyed to the local village where Mr. Thomas had a branch office. I reached for the beautiful brass knocker on the front door and knocked. I was soon greeted by the receptionist dressed in a spotless white uniform who escorted me to the drawing room. I fiddled with my cap, tried to look intelligent and hoped that my new hero would arrive, but after a long wait—five minutes!—Mr. Thomas came in. He was short, square-shouldered with slash-back grey hair, bushy eyebrows and dressed, as always, in a brown jacket and riding breeches with knee length stockings. The latter was the traditional dress for a country vet, except in summer.

I saluted him, gulped, swallowed, gulped again, stood erect—all four feet of me—and nervously said. 'Sir, I want to be a vet-er-in-ary sur-geon.' There was a long pause (so it seemed) as he looked me up and down—more down than up—and then remarked 'young man, you better go home and grow a lot!'

It was a very long ride home. Even the melodious sound of a cuckoo singing in the woods on that gorgeous spring morning failed to placate my gloom. However, when I arrived, my Dad had his usual words of wisdom and consoled me, 'never mind, men are measured from the shoulders up!'

Back in school, I entered Form 4 with an ever-increasing determination to achieve my goal. I witnessed many more births on the farm including chickens hatching, calving, lambing but never a foaling. It is a well-known fact among farmers that if you are trying to keep an eye on a mare foaling, you had better not blink or you will miss it!

One day, when one of the servants went to bring the cows in for evening milking, he found old Flora, which had calved a day previously, stretched out on the field. Dad immediately called the vet and soon, here came my hero, Bob. He took out some medication and proceeded to give her an injection under the skin in the neck. In a few minutes, Flora started to move her legs and was soon on her feet. 'A miracle! A miracle!' exclaimed my Dad. Later I learned that Flora had milk fever and the calcium solution had saved her.

That was it! I wrote to the Royal Veterinary College, London and applied for admission. You can imagine my chagrin when I received a letter, a couple of weeks later, stating there would not be any vacancies until 1941. I eventually got over my disappointment and wrote to the Royal (Dick) Veterinary College, Edinburgh, Scotland. I was accepted for the 1939 autumn term, subject to meeting academic requirements.

I went back to school for the final year—Form 5. This turned out to be a tough one but I had been forewarned by my brothers! We were assigned lots of homework to prepare for the dreaded Central Welsh Board (CWB) Examination at the end of the summer term. The tests lasted for most of the week with the papers set by external examiners appointed by the Board. In order to get into college, it was essential for me to do well in this examination. My classmates and I breathed a sigh of relief when it was over, yet with sadness that it was also the parting of the ways.

The summer of 1938 I spent at home helping on the farm—playing cricket with my brothers on the meadow whenever Dad ran out of jobs for us—unless Mam assigned us to build a rockery, where she grew beautiful flowers, or mow the lawns—and do a lot of weeding! With all the usual rain, the latter was always a problem. On wet days we played darts, rings, snakes and ladders, or card games. As the season progressed, we had lots of apples, pears, plums, and new potatoes and vegetables. My mouth still waters at the thought of a meal of roast lamb, new potatoes, carrots, french beans with lots of mint sauce and gravy. This was the summer that Henry, the other local carpenter, came and built a greenhouse. Mam was so happy when it was finished because she had waited a long time for one. Soon she had us busy filling it with tomato plants, cucumbers and some flowers. The crops from the virgin soil were abundant. Later in the season, it was time to gather blackberries which grew on the brambles on the hedgerows. On an average season we would gather enough for lots of tarts and many jars of jam or jelly.

To earn some pocket money we set traps to catch moles. We would take their skins, nail them on a board to dry and then sell them for 2d (two pence) each. We were also allowed to try our luck at trapping rabbits but not for sale—Mam made delicious rabbit pies. The rabbits were so numerous that Dad would sell the rights to the local rabbit trapper. On an occasional summer's evening, Ellis, from a neighbouring farm, would come by with his greyhound and we had a lot of fun watching him hunt rabbits in a couple of fields which had a lot of brush.

This was far from being the machinery age on the farm and Dad had some very fine majestic Shire horses named Capten, Duchess and Bess. Nancy, our Welsh cob, was also our milk pony. Every morning, John, our oldest servant would harness her in the milk cart, load the milk churns and away they would go to the local creamery. When I became old enough to deliver the milk on my own I felt like a king as Nancy and I drove through the village.

The month of August seemed like an eternity, but the postman finally brought the much awaited results of the CWB examination, which were published in the *Western Mail* the national newspaper, each year at the end of the month. I nervously scanned for the results for Whitland Grammar School—and lo, right at the end of the alphabet was my name—ERIC IDWAL WILLIAMS. That was, indeed, a summer to remember because, along with many of our neighbours, we had a telephone and electricity installed. The old Hurricane oil lamps were finally put away.

Meanwhile, the clouds of war were slowly gathering over Europe. Germany had been humiliated by defeat in World War I and by the early 1930s, inflation was rampant and there was much political unrest. It was a perfect situation for the totalitarian ideology of Adolph Hitler, a young radical of Austrian birth. He managed to rouse the German people by his vitriolic oratory and visions to build a super German race. He organized a Nazi (National Socialist) Party which gradually gained strength until January 1933, when Hitler became Chancellor of Germany. By the end of the decade the Nazis had built very formidable military forces and in March 1938, their forces invaded Austria and soon threatened Czechoslovakia. This resulted in the Munich Conference with the outcome that the Prime Ministers of Britain and France gave in to Hitler by persuading the Czechs to give up Sudetenland with its predominantly German population. Neville Chamberlain, the British Prime Minister flew back to London Airport where he waved the famous (or infamous) white paper declaring 'peace in our time.' Chamberlain has been much maligned by historians but at least Britain had 'a wake-up call' to start preparing for war.

For me, there were some very good things. I was informed that a vacancy had occurred and was offered entry to the London College in 1939, provided I passed my CWB examination (which I did).

I went back to school but now into Form 6 where I studied chemistry, physics, and biology. I was really biding my time until I could enter college. The change of academic pace was welcome after the vigour of Form 5, but work on the farm did not let up. I had to get up early and help with the milking, by hand, take a quick breakfast and race off to catch the school bus.

Life in Form 6 turned out to be enjoyable, and rather relaxed—with no pressure from terminal examinations. Also I was concentrating on subjects that would better prepare me for the first year of college.

Soon, spring arrived with lots of interesting activities on the farm—sheep lambing and also the calving season. A sure sign of spring was the arrival of the cuckoo. These migrating birds spend winters in the southern hemisphere and, along with the swallows, come back usually in April. To hear the voice of a cuckoo echoing through the valley was an absolute delight. My brothers and I always had a competition over who would see the first cuckoo. Haymaking started towards the end of May or early June but often much later in wet weather. The scent of new mown meadow hay to this day brings on a great feeling of nostalgia, probably more than anything else I know.

The summer term came to an end and once again I said goodbye to my teachers and fellow students because now I knew that I was leaving to go to college—but not quite!

Life in general was gradually changing. The news from Europe revealed that Germany was building up a huge army, air force and navy. The British government introduced conscription for able-bodied men except for those engaged in 'key' areas such as farmers, veterinary surgeons, doctors, etc. The summer of 1939 was glorious with bumper crops of hay, vegetables and fruit. We spent several afternoons on the beach at Pendine and the highlight was the annual Sunday School trip by bus to Tenby about eighteen miles down the coast. Of all the beautiful beaches that I have had the pleasure of visiting in my life, Tenby stands out among the top because her exquisite natural beauty has not been spoilt by commercialization. An added attraction is a boat ride across the bay to Caldey Island inhabited by Cistercian monks.

As summer rolled on, it became obvious that Hitler was getting ready to strike—and so it was, on Saturday, September 1, 1939, German forces invaded Poland, having signed a treaty with Stalin, the Soviet Russian dictator, that neither country would attack the other. He had tried the same tactics on Britain but it did not work because Britain and Poland had already signed a treaty.

How well I remember that fateful weekend. The weather was

beautiful and sunny just like the rest of our unusual summer. Dad had rented some land about two miles away where he grazed some sheep and heifers over the summer. On Saturday morning he sent my brothers and me to bring the sheep home. As we walked the flock through the village of Pwlltrap and along the road home, periodically the ram would collapse, breathe heavily and then, after a while, get up to join the rest of the flock. This episode was repeated several times before we reached home and told Dad about it. Dad called the vet and soon my hero came along. He diagnosed the problem as a case of liver fluke which had caused severe anaemia and weakness. He pointed out that the soft swelling under the jaw, 'bottle jaw' was a classical sign of a liver problem. He gave the ram a capsule of liquid by mouth and in a day or two it was much better and soon recovered. My hero had done it again. (The capsule was a dose of carbon tetrachloride). Now I was *really* interested in becoming a vet.

The rumbles of war escalated and Germany was given an ultimatum to withdraw from Poland, but refused. At 11:00 a.m. on Sunday morning, September 3, Prime Minister Chamberlain came on the wireless and announced that 'a state of war exists between our countries' (his words still ring in my ears). World War II had begun.

The history of Europe was about to change for ever and so was my life, at least for a while. Due to the onset of war, it was decided to evacuate the Royal Veterinary College from the heart of London to the country about 40 miles west. The result was that the autumn term was cancelled and the College would re-open in January, 1940—so, I went back to Whitland Grammar School, again!

The term was uneventful and when the Christmas holidays arrived I went home wondering if I would really go to college. I had no idea what a hazardous journey lay ahead.

A Path of Driven Snow

Among the reams of poetry I had drummed into me at Whitland Grammar School one verse came vividly back to mind as I was about to embark on my journey in life:

'Your future lies before you
Like a path of driven snow.
Be careful how you tread it,
For every step will show.'

I was scheduled to leave by train from the local village of St. Clears on Monday morning, January 17, 1940. We had had a mild autumn, but now winter came in with a vengeance. Would I get to the railway station on time? To add to my excitement about becoming a vet, one of our cows had calving difficulty on the evening before I left. She was attended by Patrick Mathew, a young vet who delivered the calf with professional ease. However, I was very homesick and stayed awake for a long time on that Sunday night—excited and apprehensive about the journey ahead. After all, a trip to the county town of Carmarthen, ten miles away, was a rare occasion, and here was I, barely seventeen years old, about to leave a wonderful, happy home for the big wide world. I never even imagined that the journey which unfolded the next morning would challenge my courage more than anything I have known since.

I had now grown a lot—there were all five feet and four inches of me! I had also graduated from my school cap to a trilby hat, and for the first time I had a brand new suit with long trousers (since I was the fourth in line I always wore 'hand-me-downs' from my brothers).

The great day finally arrived. Following a good breakfast of porridge, hot milk, toast and marmalade, I said goodbye to my mother, brother and sisters and to my Dad, who had been ill for a long time.

It was hard to leave them. My sister Lilwen and I eventually left for the local railway station. The roads were slippery and we drove along carefully until we reached the little village of Pwlltrap, with a street of houses on one side, one pub and our beloved Bethlehem

Congregational Chapel. Lo and behold, our old Austin car stopped and wouldn't re-start! Luckily, Joe, the local rabbit trapper, lived nearby and he very generously offered to take me to the station—so, along with my plush new luggage I bundled into his van with the rabbits, and away we went, arriving at the station just as the train was about to leave.

I was off on a 200-mile journey to the town of Reading, 40 miles west of London, where the College was now located. Due to the severe weather, the train moved along rather slowly and was detoured to Bristol and then on to the main London line. I sat in the corner of the train compartment all alone, and my mind wandered back over my life as the snowflakes whizzed by outside. I reflected on my wonderful upbringing in a loving, Christian home, with regular Chapel attendance three times on Sundays most of the time, the masterly sermons from the pulpit—though 45 minutes were sometimes more than I could endure, and I received many a nudge from my mother for fidgeting or sniggering at the deacons who shouted *Amen* as the preacher reached his crescendo! The Chapel was undoubtedly the religious and social centre of our life. On Saturday mornings, we attended Band of Hope led by our Minister, the Revd. Eiddig Jones. On Wednesday evenings the Young Peoples' Guild met for fellowship, present plays and prepare for our annual *Eisteddfod* .

I recalled wonderful Miss Lewis and Headmaster Morgan Thomas, the characters on that two-mile journey to school and the superb teachers at Whitland Grammar School.

I was going to miss my brothers in particular. All those pillow fights, constant arguing during cricket and soccer games on the meadow, being caught smoking tuppenny Woodbines, which made us very sick, and getting marched off to bed for our crime; picnics on the beach, getting up in the night to check the sheep at lambing time, the nostalgic scent of new-mown hay, milking cows in the early morning, and then a quick breakfast and dashing off to catch the school bus, and the family singsongs around the fire on some cold winter nights and Sunday evenings with sister Ceinwen at the piano. She played the organ at our chapel for over 40 years. Her life was centred around our family and Chapel. The verse that comes to my mind so well personifies her life: *Blessed are the pure in heart for they shall see God.*

The train eventually reached Swindon station. Here, I spent two long, cold hours before the connecting train finally came along and took us to Reading. It was now late evening, the journey having taken over ten hours. My cousin, Rees Evans, who was a third year student, was supposed to meet me, but I was all alone. I had no choice other than to take a taxi—my maiden voyage! I piled in with enough luggage for an ambassador, and away we went, skidding and rolling along the icy streets in the blackout (due to the war) in quest of my digs. The taxi driver had never heard of the street so eventually he pulled up to ask the lonely pedestrian if he knew the way. I couldn't believe it—he was my cousin, also looking for my destination! He jumped in, and eventually we found it on London Road, near Sutton's seed research centre, the home of Mr. and Mrs. George Hawkins. I went to bed tired and *very* homesick.

My first day in 'exile' was spent enrolling at Reading University, where classes for the first two years of College would now be held. I also toured some of the awesome city and then returned to my digs for a quiet evening by the fire and awaited the arrival of two students who would be my classmates, Richard Knowles and John Warde. They arrived, but quite unexpectedly, so did my cousin who broke the news to me that my Dad had passed away. My whole world collapsed, and my dreams were shattered, but I was also relieved—since I was going home again. There are no feelings to compare in any way with the horror of homesickness.

The journey home the next day was not remarkable in spite of the weather. The snow had fallen heavily at home since I left, and once again we experienced the wonderful kindness and togetherness of our neighbours, who cleared the road from the farm to the highway for the funeral.

I was home for a week and then I had to start out again. Would destiny be kinder to me this time? The snow had remained, and the road was like a skating rink as my Uncle Tom drove me to Carmarthen station, ten miles away. I had to take an early morning train which did not stop at our village.

We arrived at the station safely, and I took off once again. The train took the same detour, and by mid-day the weather had become very hazardous. Our pace became slower and slower, and eventually, when we reached Wootton Bassett, there was an announcement, 'Passengers, please disembark and transfer to buses which are waiting to take you to Swindon Station.' The snow drifts now had made it impossible for the train to proceed further. The ten-mile bus ride froze my feet and numbed my brain, and soon we arrived at the all too familiar waiting room at Swindon Station, where I almost froze during my first journey, but at least this time they had hot drinks and sandwiches for sale. Two hours later, a snow-covered train arrived which took us the rest of our journey to Reading. This time it had taken twelve hours to get there. The station was almost empty, and the buses and taxis had stopped running.

I picked up my luggage—this time only a small suitcase and walked in quest of my lodgings again. In spite of my rather unique ability to lose my way (which I found out later in life) I managed to trek along the blacked-out streets of Reading in deep snow to my destination with relative ease. Destiny had been kind to me after all.

I crawled into bed, tired, apprehensive, homesick, but reminding myself, 'A Welshman never, never gives up.'

My college life was about to begin and I woke early the next morning. I donned my long, dark overcoat and trilby hat and walked to the University—along the avenue, past a cemetery, two pubs, a hospital and finally, after a two-mile hike, I reached the University. Now, where on earth in this massive institution, with all its cloisters, was my classroom? After much tramping along and head scratching, I remembered, 'Fortune favours the brave' and ventured into a classroom. I knocked on the door and walked in. I found myself confronted by a class of youthful characters facing Dr. George Clough, a gentleman who fitted every bit my mental picture of a college professor—rotund, almost bald, wearing a bow-tie and rimless eyeglasses.

'Please, Sir,' I enquired in my broad Welsh accent, 'is this where the vet-er-in-ary students meet for Chemistry class?'

'Yes,' he replied with a supercilious air, 'who are you?'

'Will-iams, Sir,' I replied, squeezing my trilby hat.

The noble gentleman took out his shining gold watch from his waistcoat pocket and with a destructive air declared, 'Young man, you are a week and a quarter of an hour late!'

I climbed the steps to the back of the class, pulled out a notebook and pencil, and joined the chemistry class. My real journey had just begun.

"Young man — you are a week and a quarter of an hour late!"

The First Six Months

The cold hard winter continued, and the war in Europe was raging. There was no time for extracurricular activities because the delay in starting classes until January meant that we still had to complete our first academic year by early July. Classes started at 9:00 a.m., but Wednesday afternoons were free after 1:00 p.m. The usual three ten-week terms were condensed to fit this schedule. Having spent a year in Grammar School studying science courses, I found the chemistry, physics and biology classes interesting and not too challenging, but the volume of work was far more than I had been used to—and our Grammar School schedule was no picnic, either!

I bought a bicycle for ten shillings and rode to classes and back, a distance of about two miles each way. There was little traffic, except trams, since petrol rationing was already in force. The streets were dark at night, and all buildings were blacked-out so as to emit as little light as possible. Car headlamps were fitted with special devices to cut down the amount of light. Everyone carried a gas mask strapped over the shoulder and an I.D. card. It was an offence not to carry them.

On Saturdays, my fellow lodgers and I would assist our landlord, George, on his allotment as soon as Spring arrived. The City of Reading allocated segments of land for householders to grow vegetables, mainly potatoes, carrots, peas, french beans, radish, lettuce, beetroot, and parsnips. This was a vital part of the war effort where there was an urgent need to produce as much food as possible. This became abundantly clear when Germany launched the dreaded U-boats which laid magnetic mines in an attempt to annihilate us.

After six months of classes and laboratories in three ten-week terms, with a week off for Easter and Whitsun, we reached our final examinations period. At the end of the first and second terms we had terminal examinations of three hours in each subject, when we were required to answer any six out of eight questions. True/False and multiple-choice questions were unheard of throughout my professional training. The finals were tough and conducted by external examiners appointed by the Royal College of Veterinary Surgeons, our governing body. They consisted of three-hour written examinations, which were graded before we took our oral and practical examinations a few days later. For better or for worse, throughout my five years of college, the examination results were posted shortly after I finished my assignments since my name was at the end of the alphabet; it was a relief to have it over so soon. There had been one significant change in that the examiners used to stay and visit with the candidates after the results were posted until one year, several students failed to pass. They were so mad that the examiner, whom the students thought was responsible for it, was thrown into a water tank! From then on, it was not suprising that the examiners left before the results were announced.

I returned home after completing my first year, having passed my finals with honours. However, it was also a sad occasion, for life on the home hearth would never be the same again without Dad. His stately figure was sorely missed in the home, community and the chapel. By his shrewd judgement and eye for an animal the Grove herd of British Friesans under the name of J.T. Williams & Sons was well set to reach national fame.

Mam and my brothers, Dyfrig and Iorwerth, were running the farm along with sisters Ceinwen and Lilwen and three farm servants. Brother Awstin left Barclays Bank where he was employed and enlisted in the Royal Navy. Brother Huw was still at the Grammar School. Farming was a top priority industry now, and each farm was assessed a quota of acres for growing corn, which meant wheat, barley, and oats. (The term corn was used for Indian corn, which we fed to the chickens mainly).There was also a quota for potatoes. Fertilizers and limestone were made available for the land at moderate prices, and the slogan now was 'Grow two blades of grass where one used to'. There was a major difference in the farm operation—with a new Fordson tractor and a milking machine. I spent my holiday working on the farm.

To provide longer working time for farmers, double summer time was produced. The clocks were advanced two hours, which meant daylight almost until midnight. It was great for the harvest but impossible to get the children and the chickens to bed!

Besides working long hours on the farm, most young farmers volunteered for Home Guard duty with training sessions mainly on Sundays. They also took turns at check points set up at various locations on the main roads.

Another significant factor was the establishment of the Women's Land Army. Thousands of young women, mostly from urban areas, volunteered their services and were housed in camps in various parts of the United Kingdom. They showed a remarkable ability to cope with farm work and contributed enormously to the war effort especially during haymaking, corn harvest, and planting and gathering the potato crops.

A large number of children were evacuated from the London area and other large cities and were assigned to farms and private homes in rural areas. They learned that milk came from cows and not from a bottle! It was fascinating to observe how these evacuees adapted to their new way of life. In our area, they soon picked up the Welsh language. It was a real treat to hear them recite verses at our chapel with a cockney accent!

The war brought a totally new perspective for the veterinary profession, which emerged from the low key 'horse doctor' image to a

A Carmarthen area Home Guard unit comprised mainly of farmers.
(*Photo courtesy of Home Guardsman Douglas Harries.*)

A vibrant group of the Women's Land Army stationed near Llandeilo.
(*Photo courtesy of WLA member Margaret Rushton Harries.*)

vital link in animal health and food production. A nationwide scheme was launched to eradicate tuberculosis (TB) in cattle with vets carrying out TB tests on their clients' cattle herds. They were certified 'clean' (TB free) after a final test by a Ministry of Agriculture vet. A real incentive was an extra two pence per gallon of milk from TB free herds.

Vets also learned the latest methods for the treatment and control of cattle diseases and reproductive problems. Their expertise contributed enormously to improving animal health and food productivity. Very soon a new method for breeding cattle was introduced in the form of artificial insemination (AI). Over the years, AI has been invaluable in the control and eradication of reproductive diseases and to the improvement of livestock world wide. A new vaccination programme to control contagious abortion in cattle was initiated. Known as brucellosis or Bang's disease, this was a major problem in an infected herd, causing abortion and the subsequent loss in milk production and often sterility. It can also cause undulant fever in human beings. A new vaccine was used on adult cattle but with only limited success. Eventually a vaccine was developed which was inoculated into calves and proved to be very successful.

Meanwhile, the war in Europe, which had been relatively calm over the winter, erupted with fury when Germany invaded Norway and Denmark in April, 1940. Both countries fell to the Nazis in a few weeks. There was growing disillusionment in Britain over this grave turn of events and especially with the leadership—or more precisely, the lack of leadership by Prime Minister Neville Chamberlain. He eventually resigned under pressure in May, and Winston Churchill took the helm. The whole concept of national pride and resolution

Fred Sage, a London evacuee, rides the horse during haymaking time at Harry Jeremy's (standing) farm. (*Photo courtesy of Nansi Jeremy.*)

changed dramatically under his dynamic leadership. Germany invaded Holland and Belgium on May 10. They collapsed in a few days, and so did the much-heralded French Maginot line, supposedly built to keep out the German invader, but the gate was left open when the Nazis circumvented it from the north via Belgium. The British Expeditionary Force, which had landed in France soon after the outbreak of war had to retreat to the coast where a flotilla of destroyers, mine sweepers, torpedo boats, private yachts and motor boats snatched to safety over 300,000 troops (including 100,000 French) across the English Channel to the south-east of England. This daring feat became known as the 'miracle of Dunkirk.'

We were now living under the constant threat of invasion. Germany signed an armistice treaty with France in June, and apparently Hitler expected Britain to follow suit—not so, for under Churchill's dogged leadership Britain braced herself with determination to dig in. Hitler decided on 'Operation Sea Lion,' which was a planned invasion of Britain. In what became known as 'The Battle of Britain,' he let loose the fury of the Luftwaffe on August 12. Waves of bombers attacked selected targets mainly in the south-east of England. The Royal Air Force was vastly outnumbered but fought valiantly. It reached a stage one day when every possible fighter was in the air in a desperate effort to beat off the enemy. They held their own, and the enemy was vanquished—for the time being, at least, causing Hitler to turn on Russia.

Winston Churchill paid tribute to the gallant men of the Royal Air Force with his immortal words:

'Never in the annals of human conflict was so much owed by so many to so few.'

Churchill continued to rouse the nation and her allies with thundering eloquency including:

'I have nothing to offer but blood, toil, sweat and tears' when he became Prime Minister in 1940.

'We shall defend our Island, whatever the cost may be. We shall fight on the beaches, we shall fight on the landing grounds, we shall fight in the fields and in the streets. We shall fight in the hills, we shall never surrender.'

On his visits to factories, bombed areas and military operations, Churchill's 'V for Victory' sign was a great stimulus.

In 1946 at Fulton, Missouri he delivered the famous speech in which he declared:

'From Stettin in the Baltic to Trieste in the Adriatic, an iron curtain has descended across the continent.'

John Brown's Fair, Carmarthen. This was an annual event in the spring when farmers came to trade horses. The Fair was named after a Deputy Mayor who initiated it in the mid 1800s.

In the autumn a Michaelmas Fair was held in several towns, along with the annual Pleasure Fair. Here farmers would come to search for servants and maids for the following year. As a gesture of goodwill he gave his new employee two shillings, which was referred to as ' earn'. If the servant or maid did not come, the 'earn' was expected to be returned!

Seeing Practice

I returned to College in September (1940) to continue my studies. I also changed my 'digs' to the home of Jack and Nellie White across the street. There was now quite a difference in our class. A few of my first-year classmates had joined the Armed Forces, and several new students joined us. They had opted to stay in school and get exemption from the first year by studying for and passing the Higher Certificate matriculation examination in the required subjects of chemistry, physics, and biology.

Our curriculum now included histology and embryology, which dealt with the development and structure of the animal body, and physiology, which is a study of body function. I found both subjects to be very interesting, though the amount of classwork was enormous even by comparison with the first year. I was absolutely intrigued and, along with my classmates, overawed by our instructor in embryology and histology, namely Dr. Emmanual Cyprian Amoroso. He was a West Indian with a superb command of the English language and his subject matter. His nickname was 'Amo' and his brilliant lectures on the development of the foetal membranes are still vivid in my mind.

Our physiology course was highlighted by laboratory sessions two afternoons a week, conducted by Dr. Rosenberg. We were endeared by his charming broken English accent, but poor old 'Rosy' was not the best at helping us when we messed up our attempt to record muscle function in frogs on the old carbon drums—we probably had more carbon on us than on the drums! The academic year was now back on schedule, namely three terms of 10 weeks each, with a month's holiday for Christmas and Easter.

I spent most of the summer of 1941 at home, and now there was an even greater need to increase food production. Even though Hitler turned his guns towards Russia, the dreaded German U-boats and the magnetic mines continued to cause heavy losses to the British merchant fleet.

Whenever we discuss weather we usually say, 'If it is not raining, it is going to!' That's how it was during that summer, so I decided it would be a good time for me to start seeing practice with the local vets. Each veterinary student was required to spend at least six months with a vet in practice before being eligible to graduate. The assignment could be spread over several holiday periods. The student was also required to present a case record file, which had to include a report on at least six cases of dystocia in cattle, at the final examination.

I spent all my assignments at the practice established by Mr. Roger Thomas in the late '20s in Carmarthen, the county town. The town dates back to Roman times under the name Maridunum. It is a very prosperous market town for produce and livestock, on the banks of the Tywi river.

The price of cattle steadily increased. How well do I recall, in the 1930s, Dad selling a dairy cow (freshly calved) at the mart for less than £20, and the cattle dealer who went round the farms buying cull cattle (old and/or barren) for as little as he could! (His favourite bid was 'a pound a leg'). It created quite a stir when a pedigree Dairy Shorthorn bull was sold for 100 guineas at a farm sale.

There was also a dramatic change in livestock, especially dairy cattle. The Dairy Shorthorn had been the predominant breed hitherto, but now, with a great emphasis on increasing milk production, the British Friesian breed started to take over. My father's vision in 1912 was now paying off handsomely. The Grove herd was well-established and soon reached national fame with a great demand for young bulls from the herd. My brothers had obviously inherited Dad's good judgment of cattle and eventually built up the herd to win the gold cup for the best dairy herd in England and Wales in 1995 and 1996.

From the vet's point of view, this crossbreeding (Friesian and Shorthorn) created calving problems. There were many dystocias (difficult birth) due to oversized calves. In those days, the vet had to deliver them by traction since Caesarean surgery was rarely attempted, due to a law requiring general anaesthesia for such and other major surgeries. The available anaesthetics, mainly chloroform, ether by inhalation or chloral hydrate intravenously were not well tolerated. A cow lying on her side is constantly in danger of accumulating large volumes of gases not being able to escape (A normal cow produces over a litre of stomach gases a minute, which is regularly expelled by eructation or belching).

The result, rather too often, was that the calf could not be delivered by vagina and it would die. This meant doing an embryotomy in part—such as removing one forelimb or total removal systematically in various sections; this could be a very strenuous operation for several hours.

I thoroughly enjoyed seeing practice and returned to college full of enthusiasm. I was now in the third year, (September 1941) and classes were held in Home Park, a mansion two miles from Reading, near the village of Sonning-on-Thames. The College had acquired a lease on this property, which had several stables and farmland. Our classroom was a large hut in the adjacent woods. This was the year when we studied anatomy, which included the complete dissection of a horse, over the three terms. The horse was still the 'standard' animal in the teaching of anatomy. The other domesticated animals' anatomy was studied on a comparative basis (these included cattle, sheep, pigs, dogs, and cats). Our laboratory was a stall per animal in the stable! My dissection partner was John Rowe, a very tall, bushy-haired fellow from Devon. We called him 'Tiny'. We often had meat fights with our fellow students when things became rather boring! Our instructor was the renowned Professor James (Jimmy) McCunn. He was appointed Professor of Anatomy in 1926 and developed an extensive consultation practice, being particularly noted for his skill as an expert witness in courts of law. A stately figure, he always wore a bowler hat, and students and colleagues alike turned to him in time of trouble. His blackboard drawings, one felt, were too good to erase, proving the value of the blackboard and chalk method of teaching. He was also a medical doctor and was the epitome of a true scholar, an aristocrat who cared for his students and professional colleagues. He had a very able assistant in Dr. C.W. Ottoway (Oscar).

We also studied veterinary hygiene which covered animal nutrition, management, farm operations, design of farm buildings and pasture management. Professor W. R. Miller was a walking encyclopaedia in these subjects which he expounded with a rich Scottish accent. He was aided in teaching nutrition by the sedate Dr. Muir, known also for wearing the same suit day in day out!

A very interesting course during this academic year was Animal Management taught by Dr. N. J. Scorgie. He also was a Scot. Since this was still the age of the horse, students were 'drilled' in two main areas: how to tell the age of a horse, and the proper way to describe the markings of a horse, including measuring its height—with a special stick from the foot to the withers (base of the neck) expressed in hands, one hand being 4 inches. Undoubtedly, the most interesting area was the instruction on how to tell the age of a horse. This is quite an art based mainly on tooth eruption times, shape of the tooth (table), the angle of appostion of the upper and lower incisor (front) teeth when viewed from the side, and others such as the seven year notch and Galvayne's groove. After some experience, the student was expected to be able to tell fairly accurately up to the age of 12 years. A horse's front teeth become longer with age, hence the term 'getting long in the tooth.'

The RVC Soccer team.

Another area of instruction centred on the proper method for the examination of a horse, including recording the proper description of colour markings, age, height, and any obvious blemishes.

Probably the most unattractive or boring subject was pharmacology, the study of drugs, their chemical composition and dosage for the various domestic animals. It demanded a lot of memory work. This was the era before antibiotics and the sulpha drugs, except for sulphapiridine which became well-known for its use when Winston Churchill developed pneumonia. There were very few pre-packaged drugs so our curriculum also involved instruction in preparing various prescriptions. A real 'must' was to know how to write a prescription properly.

I went home for the Christmas holiday and went to see practice as usual at Carmarthen. My cousin Rees, who had qualified and was engaged in the practice, used to tease me often about not having a girlfriend—and I would say, 'Well, why don't you find one for me?' To my surprise he arranged for me to talk to his girlfriend's sister on the telephone. We agreed to go on a blind date to the pictures. The main film was entitled 'Caught in a Draught'—and that's all I remember about it, but Mary Harries, the lovely farmer's daughter, and I did 'hit it off' and would meet again!

So I went back to my studies. I remained in my lodgings in Reading and cycled to my classes at Sonning, two miles away. I played soccer for our College on Saturday afternoons against local teams and military units in the area. The home team always entertained the visitors with tea and sandwiches after the game. The war news was not good, with food and petrol rationing in force. Queuing at grocery and other stores became a regular ritual for housewives. This was brought home to me when my landlady asked me to get some cat food, for which I stood in line for quite a while. In the evenings, we would go out and look towards London, about 40 miles away—the sky was lit up very often with fires from the relentless bombing.

There was however, some shining lights amidst all the gloom— namely the voice of the lovable Vera Lynn as she sang *The White Cliffs of Dover*, *A Nightingale in Berkeley Square* and many other favourites on the wireless while entertaining troops and factory workers. She became known as 'The Forces Sweetheart'—to all of us—and who could ever forget Glenn Miller and his band's rendition of *In the Mood* and above all, the booming, heart-warming oratory of Winston Churchill over the wireless?

The Summer of 1942 was spent mostly at the local practice which had grown considerably due to the ever-increasing demand for veterinary services. There were two new vets, namely, Morgan Wynne and George Davies. They worked very hard and expected the same effort from me and the other students who came to see practice—there was hardly time to chase the girls! It was very difficult to obtain good motorcars. I cannot count the number of times we had to crank the engine or push the car down the road in neutral, jump in and quickly flip her in gear!

A specific assignment for students, in between farm calls, was to prepare a stock of medicines for each vehicle and for clinic use. There were very few prepackaged medicines from the pharmaceutical companies, so we prepared them. Among the most common medications was the cleansing drench which we prepared by mixing the following with a pestle and mortar;

½ oz nux vomica

½ oz ammonium carbonate

½ oz ginger

8 ozs magnesium sulphate (Epsom's salts)

These ingredients after thorough mixing were packaged in newspaper since cardboard cartons were not available.

This medication was prescribed to be given as a drench in a quart of water. It was often given to freshly calved cows to cleanse the system, or for digestive problems. In the latter cases, there was a 'follow-up' of the same medication in divided doses, twice a day for three days.

The method of drenching had not changed over the years—the medication was mixed with a quart or pint of water in a bottle with a long neck. With an assistant holding the animal's head steady (or at least trying to) the bottle was introduced towards the back of mouth and the medication administered slowly. Unfortunately, in some instances, it went down the wrong way, namely the trachea (wind pipe) and into the lungs—resulting in drenching pneumonia or sometimes sudden death. Eventually, the stomach tube was used for this purpose and in this case the medication was mixed with a half a bucket of water. The tube was passed through the nose into the gullet (food pipe) and down into the stomach. The medication was either pumped into the stomach via the tube or allowed to gravitate by holding the bucket a couple of feet above the animal's head. Here again there were accidents when an inexperienced person passed the tube into the trachea and lungs by mistake.

Medicating a horse was a lot different. Because of anatomical factors, drenching a horse was not done. Instead, medication was prepared as a bolus in a gelatin capsule with rounded ends. To administer the bolus, we used a narrow, flexible stick about 2 feet long, pointed at one end, which was inserted about ½ inch into one end of the bolus. The next procedure was to pull out the horse's tongue over the side of the face and then, with a quick combined effort, thrust the bolus, on the stick, to the back of the mouth, then withdraw the stick and release the tongue simultaneously. Eventually a balling gun was used.

Every student was horrified when called to do this in front of a client—who would rib him if the horse spit out the chewed bolus. Likewise, a client often challenged students to tell the age of his horse—and woe to us if we were wide of the mark! It became top priority to master both medication methods and ageing. The bolus was later replaced by the stomach tube, especially for administering worm medicine to young horses. I should also add that most were Shire horses, over 16.2 hands in height.

Streatley House

The remaining two years of our curriculum were spent at Streatley-on-Thames about twelve miles west of Reading. This delightful, picturesque village is in the county of Berkshire. It is connected by a bridge over the river Thames with Goring-on-Thames, in Oxfordshire, also a very beautiful village. The pubs in Berkshire closed at 10:00 p.m. but not until 10:30 p.m. in Oxfordshire. Partying students made full use of both!

The headquarters of our College was Streatley House, a large square brick building of three stories. It provided office accommodation, dining and common rooms. There was also the Annex and a hostel for about 50 students. Our classroom was a large hut on the grounds of Streatley House.

Several students stayed with local residents. Ifor George and I joined a few others in a private house but the landlady was a little eccentric to say the least and had a loving obsession with cats. Soon we moved to Mrs. Hall's house. She really took great care of us for £1-7-6d a week which included full board, sandwiches for lunch and our laundry. She loved to lean on her house broom and give us all the gossip.

In addition to our classwork, we took our part in defending our country. We joined the Goring platoon of the Home Guard attached to the 4th Berkshire Regiment. Every Tuesday evening and Sunday morning, we had Home Guard duty and occasionally went on field exercises. In addition, each student was periodically assigned fire-watching duty, about two nights a month. There was an ever-present danger of incendiary bombs being dropped by the Germans.

Our courses now included pathology, the study of diseases which became one of my favourite subjects, taught by Professor Bosworth (Bosey) and Dr. E. G. White (Eg White). The course also included bacteriology with Dr. Reggie Lovell who had a part in the research and discovery of penicillin. Professor Clifford Formston, who taught surgery, was a very articulate lecturer and a meticulous surgeon. Medicine was taught by Dr. Joe Holmes, known as 'enema Joe,' until

Professor Harry Burrows took over in our final year. In accordance with British law, students (and others not licensed) were not allowed to perform surgery on live animals. Our experience in this area was thus confined to observing the surgeon in action. Often there was a group of us and short ones like myself usually did not have a good view!

Albert Messervy taught obstetrics and reproductive diseases. He was a strong, square shouldered vet who managed to escape from his practice on the island of Jersey before the Germans took over. Parasitology was taught by dear Dr. Oldham.

Our schedule continued so as to have Wednesday afternoons free. One day a group of us decided to take the train to Reading and go to the cinema. Shortly after the film started, there was a loud noise and the lights went out. We scrambled out to find that a couple of bombs had landed about two streets away. It was dropped by a German bomber being chased by R.A.F. fighters.

The bombing of Pearl Harbour by the Japanese occurred on December 7, 1941, a vicious attack, described by President Roosevelt as 'a day that will live in infamy.' This brought the United States into the war with Germany, Italy and Japan. American troops soon arrived in Britain in large numbers and the build-up for the invasion of Europe had begun. The spring of 1943 was noted for the defeat of the Axis forces in North Africa by Allied Forces.

Our classwork plus Home Guard duty continued through the spring of 1943. I spent most of the summer holidays with the local vet and gained a lot of practical experience. Our clinical studies had reached a stage where I was now able to participate more in the diagnosis of the various diseases encountered in the practice. However, I went home periodically to work on the farm and help out with the harvest. This was before the coming of the combine. After the corn (wheat, oats, or barley) was cut by the reaper or binder, it was quite a tedious job to stack the sheaves in groups of 4 or 6 depending on the crop. Several camps for German and Italian prisoners-of-war had been set up across the country. They were sent out in groups to work on farms whenever requests were received from the farmers. Some were assigned to individual farms. Umberto, an Italian, worked on our farm for a few years. He was strong and conscientious but he enjoyed to sow his wild oats with the local village girls!

In view of the usually wet weather with the corresponding loss of the hay harvest, a totally new concept was introduced. Rather than wait for the usual haymaking season, the grass was cut at a much earlier stage and harvested the next day as silage in special circular silos, above ground which later gave way to pit silos.

Streatley House: *photo by Rhian Williams.*

Photo by Rhian Williams.

The Light at the End of the Tunnel

The fifth and final year rolled on and my ultimate goal was in sight. The final term in the Spring of 1944 was devoted to intensive studying for the finals along with our military duties. It became obvious that D-Day could not be far away because the countryside was alive with military vehicles and troop movements—then, on June 6 it happened—and the countryside had truly evacuated!

The first week in July was our D-Day—conquering the finals in a week of written, oral and practical examinations.

July 4, 1944—the ordeal was over! I had finally reached my goal—I qualified! As soon as the results were posted, we were instructed to gather at Goring Parish Hall where we took the oath and were admitted as Members of the Royal College of Veterinary Surgeons (M.R.C.V.S.).

So, Eric Idwal Williams. M.R.C.V.S. aged 21, collected his belongings and left for the railway station for the triumphant trip home.

As the train speeded west, I pondered over my academic journey—from elementary and grammar schools and through college. I had been blessed with a wonderful Christian home and truly dedicated teachers throughout. In college we lacked sophisticated equipment and classrooms, but due to excellent teaching of the basic subjects and down-to-earth practical approach by the clinical faculty, I felt that I was well prepared for general practice. We had been reminded many times that very often 'it won't be like the textbook describes it.' Above all, I recall we were told what would be our greatest asset, 'the best equipment you will ever have are your eyes—use them!'

From the medication aspect, there was a woeful lack of drugs for specific diseases. However, the sulpha drugs were emerging and Alexander Fleming's discovery of penicillin in the 1930s was now being pursued vigorously and became available towards the end of the 1940s.

In the absence of these drugs, it was instilled into us the importance of Tender Loving Care. Throughout my career it often made the difference.

The train steamed into St. Clears Station where I had started my journey in the snow. Now, there was the sweet smell of new-mown hay, flowers in bloom and the sun was shining.

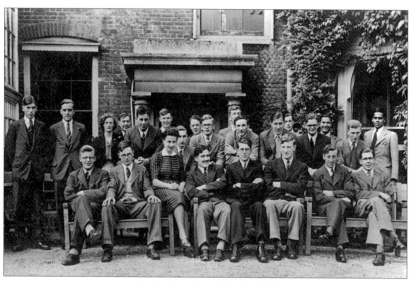

Graduating class; July 4, 1944.
(*Photo taken at Streatley House.*)

A Rude Awakening

I was lying in bed feeling as if I had the world by the tail. A few days earlier on July 4, 1944, I had qualified at the age of 21 years. It was a wonderful feeling and I dreamed of the great challenges that lay ahead.

Little did I know that the harsh reality of it all was to dawn on me within a few minutes, for my brother came charging into the bedroom and literally pulled me out of bed! 'Come on, quick, our cows are dying! I turned them into *Parc-y-goeden* and some of them are already down.'

I might explain that our home farm had about two hundred acres and every field had its own name. My Dad had started the herd in 1911 and Mother and two of my brothers had taken over after his death. The cattle had been carefully selected and bred for good conformation and high milk production. It was vitally important that they received the best care.

I shot out of bed and half-dressed ran out to the field. It was a shocking sight—three were dead and six others were so full they were about to burst. They had been turned on to a new pasture with a lot of clover.

This was a young crop which had grown rapidly due to hot and rainy days during the past week. Such pasture is also very luscious and cows are no different from people when given the opportunity—they tend to overeat! Now, any normal ruminant, such as a cow, produces large volumes of gases as a result of fermentation of food in the rumen or first stomach. In fact, this is usually about one-and-one-half to two litres per minute after a normal meal. However, this is no problem for the gases are expelled via the mouth at regular intervals. I might add that belching is a normal, 'socially accepted' practice as far as cows are concerned. Just stand and observe any normal cow and you can hear 'the music' as she gurgles or 'burps' to her heart's content!

Due to the fact that our cows had engorged themselves on the palatable young grass and the unusually high rapid gas production that also occurs under these circumstances, the cows were not able to cope with the situation. To make things worse, fresh clover pastures also contains saponin, or soap-like compounds, which cause an increase in surface tension in the stomach contents. This means that the gases are not released so readily and thus accumulate in small bubbles mixed with the food in the stomach. The result is that the stomach gets distended due to the failure to get rid of the gases and the cow's belly just gets bigger and bigger causing great pressure until she may suffocate.

When there is a real emergency, it is no use 'fiddling while Rome is burning'. I have always been inclined toward the motto 'Fortune favours the brave' or 'A faint heart never won a fair maiden'. So, here was my test! Since I had only just graduated, I might have felt I had a lot of knowledge but no instruments whatsoever. Here was a really challenging situation. Had that mighty Professor not preached the importance of asepsis and sharp, sterilized instruments as essentials of professional surgical performance?! But Mam's cows were dying and so, I borrowed my brother's pocketknife and proceeded to make a deep incision through the very tight skin and muscles into the first stomach of the nearest victim which could hardly stand up due to her over distended stomach. The incision into the stomach immediately

The field at Grove Farm where the bloat occurred, with Llangynin Church in the background.

released huge volumes of stomach contents mixed with gases. My brother, standing several feet away, was drenched by the massive spray as it shot out through the incision.

In all, six cows were given this drastic treatment. It looked like a battlefield. Since I had no instruments I sent my brother to ask my hero, Bob Morgan the vet, to come and help me. However, he was out on call, so his assistant, Morgan Wynne came and he assured my mother that her 'blue-eyed' boy had done the right thing!

We cleaned up the wounds and sutured the stomach, muscles and skin of each affected animal. Mother never believed the miracle of the clover field but by rather prompt, if unorthodox action, six of her very valuable cows had been saved. There are *certain* times when the books have to be set aside and action has to be taken in accordance with the demands of the situation. Nothing else in the world would have saved the situation—the onset was so rapid. Lest others might try to emulate our deeds on a similar situation, let me warn that only under an *extreme* emergency must this radical procedure be undertaken and the incision *must* be made only in the *left* side of the animal, behind the last rib. Under different circumstances, cows will bloat or suffer distention of the stomach with gases in which prompt medication or just passing a stomach tube down the mouth or nose will give immediate relief. The vet should always be consulted in these cases.

The Golden Era

The euphoria of graduation soon gave way to the reality of starting to earn a living. I joined the practice at Carmarthen with a pay scale which was considered to be a good one at that time, namely £6 (six pounds) a week. I was assigned a car with one floor board missing—in those days one was pleased to have *any* car but one thing was true though, you could sell it at a profit! There was no scheduled time off; after all, I was the new assistant who was expected to work hard *all* the time. However, there was that wonderful feeling (when compared to modern times—1990's) where there was absolutely *no* need to carry any liability insurance. In those days, it was totally unacceptable to even think of suing anyone, let alone the doctor or the vet. There was also a great emphasis on personal appearance and dress.

My colleagues and I worked very long hours, sometimes without any sleep for a couple of days. Practice was not as the book said it was—so many cases were presented in a totally different light—just as the teachers predicted.

Probably the biggest problem for a new graduate was to gain the confidence of the clients. There were remarks such as 'I sent for the vet and not a kid!' However, hard work, professional knowledge, common sense, humour, empathy for the patient and client proved to be the glue to success. I well recall a visit to a cow that was down in the barn and surrounded by the farmer and some of his neighbours. She had been sick for several days and when the local quack couldn't save her they sent for the vet. I was the unlucky one to be assigned the call. I warned the owner that his cow was beyond hope and gave her an injection, hoping to pull off a miracle. Shortly after I left, she died—and the word soon spread around the neighbourhood that the young vet had killed her.

However, the sun also rises. A few weeks later a farmer called requesting someone to take care of a heifer that was having difficulty calving. He was in the same neighbourhood but did not have the heart to say that he did not want the 'pup' who killed his neighbour's cow! Well, I was the only one available at that time and left immediately to attend to his cow. Unaware of my reputation, I sped to the farm to find that the local quack had tried to deliver the calf. I went to work, recognized the problem and remembering what my professor had told us that when dealing with a dystocia (difficult birth) it was a case of the right push and the right pull at the right time. I proceeded to correct the malpresentation of lateral deviation of the head and neck. Soon a live calf was delivered to the embarrassment of the quack and probably the otherwise elated client. Later he turned out to be one of our best clients and I am pleased to report that quacks were soon a vanishing breed.

Petrol rationing was still in force though there was an adequate supply for essential services such as veterinary practice. However, I had a problem! Even though I tried hard to arrange my evening calls in my girlfriend's neighbourhood it did not always work out. When I joined the practice I lived with my boyhood hero, Bob Morgan and his family. His wife, Menna, was a very kind and considerate lady. She even loaned me her bicycle to go courting! It was a long trek along the

Penllwynau.

Tywi valley for six miles to Nantgaredig and then up the hill to Penllwynau farm.

About eighteen months after joining the practice, I was given the responsibility to establish a branch practice at my home town, St. Clears. This area had been an important part of the practice for many years and it was now felt that a vet should reside there. I had spent a very happy time at the Carmarthen practice and especially with the Morgan family. Their children, Robert and Ann, still call me 'Gee Gee' (we used to play 'ride them cowboys' during my rare time off!). Richard was still a baby when I left.

I was now really tied to the grindstone because I was virtually on my own although I could call on my colleagues in Carmarthen when the work load became too heavy. I was not yet married but I was very well cared for by Jack and Jane Williams and their daughter, Joan. They ran a prosperous butcher business with deliveries to neighbouring farms, as well as running a small farm.

Two great events in my life were soon to happen. Bob Morgan decided to break away from the parent practice and asked me to join

St. Clears Village.

Our Wedding Party. Brothers Iorwerth and Dyfrig; bridegroom and bride, Eleanor
Evans, bridesmaid and cousin, Douglas and Oliver, Mary's brothers.
Front: my mother and Mary's mother.

him as his junior partner: The move to St. Clears took me further away
from that lovely farmer's daughter—much too far on a bicycle! We
had been engaged for over a year, so this was it. On Thursday,
September 4, 1947, Mary Harries and I were married at Nantgaredig
Calvinistic Chapel. It was a beautiful autumn morning and as my best
man, brother Dyfrig and I drove to the wedding we were confronted
outside the village by the usual rope across the road by two local lads,
David Parry Jones and Brian Francis—who did not let us through until
we had given them the customary tip of a few shillings. There were
some more ropes on the road from the Chapel to Mary's home and
following the reception at Mary's beautiful home overlooking the
breathtaking Tywi valley we left for our honeymoon in North Wales.

We started our married life in a flat but soon my senior partner
bought a local chemist shop. Mary and I moved into the house and the
shop became the practice surgery.

Setting up a new home was quite a challenge. The effects of the war still prevailed and we needed coupons to buy everything from food to furniture.

In keeping with Dad's prescription for a wholesome life, I became involved with village civic life, serving over ten years on the School Board and twelve years on the Parish Council, with a year as Chairman. There were many times when I was called out on urgent cases from these meetings and sometimes returned for the rest of the meeting. Throughout these years of civic service, neither I nor my colleagues received any financial remuneration. My Dad had also impressed on us the difference between a statesman who votes according to his or her conscience and a politician who 'sways with the winds of public opinion,' which is often misdirected. Our family, along with most farmers, had traditionally been strong supporters of the Liberal Party and I served as chairman of the County Association.

I was also active in the local playing field committee and played soccer one season in a summer competition for our village team. We won the cup and I even managed to score a goal off the back of my head! However, my favourite sports were rugby and cricket which I followed with much enthusiasm and attended when I could get away from the practice. I maintain until this day, that these two athletic events typify the spirit of sportsmanship far more than others.

In the true tradition of our family, I remained actively involved with Bethlehem Congregational Chapel. Over the years we held some memorable organ recitals including well known national soloists. I especially enjoyed choir practice after the evening services. Over the years we sang many of the famous Welsh anthems and choruses from Handel's *Messiah*. The highlight was the annual Gymanfa Ganu (singing festival) in September when we were joined by five neighbouring chapel choirs; children in the afternoon and adults in the evening.

I was now deeply entrenched in practice activities and I had developed considerable interest in clinical research especially on the digestive system of cattle.

After several months of clinical observation every time the opportunity arose, I was able to devise a new diagnostic test for the condition known as traumatic reticuloperitonitis. This clinical disorder occurs when a foreign object such as a nail or a piece of hay baling wire, after being swallowed in the hay or feed, penetrates the wall of the reticulum or second stomach. I wrote a thesis on my findings for which I was awarded the Fellowship of the Royal College of Veterinary Surgeons (F.R.C.V.S.) in 1954. The technique became known as the 'Williams Test.' Sadly, though, it was the year my dear mother died after a long illness. Her tender loving care and constant encouragement to do our very best in life will always be cherished.

A real boost for our profession occurred when the Animal Anaesthetics Act of 1948 allowed major surgery to be performed under local or regional anaesthesia. This was the dawn of a great era which I will discuss later under 'Barnyard Surgery' (chapter 13).

This was also the period when there was a major breakthrough in the medical world. Penicillin, the first antibiotic which had been discovered by Alexander Fleming during the 1930's was now available and literally transformed overnight our ability to treat disease and for an 'umbrella' for surgical operations. There was also the availability of several new chemotherapy agents such as sulphapiridine and sulphamethazine.

My interest in clinical research continued and led to a visit for six weeks to some French vets financed by a grant from the Harry Steele-Bodger Memorial Fund of the British Veterinary Association in 1958. I returned to our busy practice until 1960 when I left for another six weeks tour, this time to the United States on a Wellcome Research Traveling Scholarship. I visited colleagues at Cornell University and the University of Pennsylvania who had similar clinical research interests. The striking feature of this tour was a visit to Oklahoma State University's College of Veterinary Medicine where Dr. E. Wynn Jones was Director of Clinical Research. He was also a graduate of the Royal Veterinary College and we played soccer in the same college team.

I returned to St. Clears and continued to work long hours. Since the practice had grown considerably, I received much more assistance from my colleagues Gwilym Lloyd, Oswyn Evans and later Lynn Lewis and Rowland Jones.

I have referred earlier to the time I spent 'seeing practice' while I was a student. It was now my turn to be the teacher! Over the years I was accompanied on my rounds by many students who kept me up-to-date with the latest information from their college, while I constantly tried to indoctrinate them in the art of clinical diagnosis. In later chapters, I focus on a selection of clinical cases with an emphasis on the teacher-student relationship.

Each summer, Mary and the children spent a couple of weeks in an apartment overlooking Tenby harbour. This delightful seaside resort is only about eighteen miles from St. Clears. The highlight was a boat trip to Caldey Island with its ancient monastery and Cistercian monks who produce perfume from the island's flowers.

Now, let me take you back through those wonderful years as I recall some of the most exciting episodes, during what my veterinary colleagues and I always refer to as the Golden Era of veterinary practice. I also learned not only to aim high but also to keep one's feet on the ground.

Tenby harbour with Caldey Island in the background.

Dylan Thomas's Studio.

The Boat House.

A Vet's Eyeview of *Under Milk Wood*

I will never forget that dismal, drizzly, cold afternoon in November, 1953 when I descended the hill in my old Ford car into the ancient township of Laugharne. A cold, wet day was nothing unusual in this part of Wales where, if it wasn't raining, it was going to! But this was a very memorable day. Dylan Thomas, the famous Welsh poet, had come home to rest. He had died of a 'brain storm' in New York City the previous week. His funeral was being held in St. Martin's Church, and the church bell tolled mournfully as it echoed against Goosegog Hill. Nestled at the foot of the bracken-covered hill, the old Gothic-style church was overflowing with people from all walks of life. Canon S. B. Williams read from the Epistle to the Corinthians:

'Now is Christ risen from the dead—
Death shall be swallowed up in victory.'

One could sense the vast congregation whispering our departed hero's immortal lines

'They shall have stars at elbow and foot
Though lovers be lost, love shall not;
And death shall have no dominion.'

A few days later I had the painful task of putting his dog to sleep. I had paid several visits to the Dylan Thomas home, The Boat House, whenever the little pet got sick. He was a cute little fellow, a mixture of breeds, but now he was a lonely soul. With his growing age he had become a little snappy and no one really wanted him. Soon he was in the land of eternal dreams and was buried high on the cliff behind the poet's home.

Though I visited the Boat House several times, I never met Dylan Thomas. His wife, Caitlin, and the children were usually around, or a friendly neighbour. The Boat House is now a national shrine tucked on the edge of a cliff overlooking one of the most beautiful natural coastlines imaginable on Carmarthen Bay.

Where is this Milk Wood that Dylan Thomas has made so famous? The setting is the ancient township of Laugharne where there must be more unusual characters per square mile than anywhere else in the world! I had known this quaint little town since my childhood when we used to drive through it on our way to Pendine Beach, a few miles west.

I had come to know the town and her people, for hardly a day went by that I did not pass through to the neighbouring farms, attend to a backyard pig with measles (erysipelas), sick cats and dogs, strays and beloved pets. Col. Wilson's huge pet, described by Dylan as *'the St. Bernard without the brandy'* was the king of them all who put the fear of death in man and beast and in me!

Under Milk Wood—a play for voices, was only completed a month before his death, though he had worked on it for nearly ten years. It is a hilarious account of a spring day in this Welsh coastal town which begins with dreams and ghosts before dawn, moves through the brilliant, noisy day of the townsfolk, and closes as the *'rain of dusk brings on the bawdy night.'*

Who are these people who are the central characters in this masterpiece?

Laugharne is steeped in history described by the poet as,

'the last example of a medieval corporation still retaining its custom; a writer's dream and a painter's heaven.'

During the 12th century, great floods in Flanders drove the Flemish people across the English Channel and many of them settled in the south-west corner of Wales. They never did become absorbed through the years into the local culture and Welsh language, but developed their own brand of English with the use of 'thee' and 'thou.' Laugharne soon became a town of two 'cultures'—the Flemish remained around the harbour with its open square, The Grist—scene of many family feuds among the Browns, Pearces, Braces, etc., of yesteryear. They were known as the 'toughs.' These were the cocklemen and women. It appears that there was so much feuding one Saturday night that the cocklebed moved across the bay, never to come back again!

Upstreet among the flowering cherry trees were the stately homes of the rich or famous people who had found their haven under Llareggyb Hill. Overlooking the harbour stands Laugharne Castle which dates back many centuries. Here Richard Hughes wrote *High Winds in Jamaica* while he was landlord of the castle which had been badly damaged in the time of Oliver Cromwell. Laugharne is probably the only town that has her own Portreeve who presides every second Monday over the Court Leet made up of the town burgesses who own strips of land along the lines of the old feudal system. The Portreeve is elected annually during Big Court night on the first Monday in October. Afterwards he is carried shoulder-high several times around the mini-Town hall and then to the local pub! The following Sunday morning, the Portreeve hosts a breakfast for local dignitaries followed by eloquent speeches. Then he leads a procession to the local church for morning service in his Sunday best suit, *Come-to-Jesus collar*, and *Hallelujah tie*, complete with his chain of office made of gold-plated cockle shells.

Dylan Thomas described Laugharne as *one castle, one church and one Rolls Royce selling fish and chips.* He was referring to a local entrepreneur who earned the title of 'Benny Chips' because he bought a beat-up Rolls and converted it into a mobile fish and chips shop— sold in the traditional newspaper with lots of salt and vinegar.

The young lad who was born in Swansea, about forty miles away, had moved to Laugharne and stayed there because,

'some like myself, just came one day, for the day, and never left; got off the bus and forgot to get on again.'

He was steeped in Welsh lore and poetry, all of which left their mark on his rich, startling imagery and driving rhythms. Though he did not speak Welsh, his brilliance with words are truly indicative of his Welsh heritage—he made the English language sing with the fervour of a Welshman.

The years have rolled by and I still chuckle when I think of

'the good, bad boys from the lonely farms,'

Polly Garter (naughty, nice girl—I probably treated her dog!), Nogood

Boyo, Mrs. Dai Bread Two and the Reverend Eli Jenkins—the epitome of the old Welsh preacher whose roaring sermons, delivered with verse and song, bounced off the chapel ceiling and moved his spellbound congregation to the Pearly Gates. Oh, to be on St. John's Hill again and gaze across the flowing tide towards the Boat House, nestled in the rugged beauty of Goosegog Hill with her carpet of daffodils, primroses, and wild red clover.

Dylan's Studio.

Crisis on the Grist

Dylan Thomas could have travelled the whole world but would never have discovered such a theatre of characters as there were right on his doorstep in Laugharne. I loved his description of the ancient township.

One unique character was Rick Siwel, a classmate in Grammar School. He was one of the most brilliant scholars I had ever known. He became a lawyer and a career destined for a Prime Minister was unfolding for him but, due to a tragic turn of events, he had to come home to run the farm. Part of his daily chores was to deliver the milk, which he had done religiously for many years. As he pushed his cart from door to door, upstreet and downstreet, with each quart of milk he delivered a pound of wisdom. I assume he must have been the most learned milkman on record—and of course, where else but in Milk Wood!

Rick's farm was situated right in the middle of this writer's dream and painter's heaven. It was to attend to one of his cows that we received an urgent call one Tuesday afternoon. We raced down the hill, past the ancient church, along the main avenue of flowering cherry trees, around a hairpin bend and down to the Grist.

Here was the town square—where the 'toughs' lived. To the north and west, the spacious square was lined with dainty, whitewashed cottages, each with a kitchen garden and in the backyard a pig or a couple of geese. To the east stood Laugharne Castle, still a majestic ruin, draped in ivy, that had endured the fury of the onslaught by Oliver Cromwell's canon brigade many centuries ago. At the foot of the castle, stretching across the southern side of the square, was the estuary.

A delightful aroma of salt and seaweed, breezing in from the bay, made an invigorating blend with the enticing smell of the mild and bitter coming from the Corporation Arms on the other side. Such beauty was for enjoyment some other time, for our attention was soon focused towards the crisis on the Grist. In the middle of the square lay our patient—a star attraction—one of Rick's Shorthorn cows. Since the farmstead was in the town, the cows had to walk to and from the

fields along the streets. It was during the trek home for the evening
milking that old Flossie collapsed. Here she was, a pathetic sight with
her head tucked beside her left shoulder. The weather was hot and
humid (that Tuesday afternoon was our summer for that year!) and her
heart could be heard pounding away almost across the Grist. School
was out for the day, so the poor creature was surrounded by young
Parsons, Braces and Browns of all shapes and sizes, together with a
gallery of locals and holiday-makers. Phipps, the local Bobby, soon
arrived. He was an impressive figure, complete with his helmet and
heavy deep blue suit. He had been here for many years, which spoke
well for his skill in handling these characters. He didn't carry a gun
and nobody else did either. A boot in the back-side went a long way!

But Phipps soon had the situation under control as the lusty kids
were shoving hard to get a grandstand view. One little brat was so
eager he toppled right over poor Flossie, ripping the seat of his
trousers.

Rick volunteered the information that Flossie had laid down a
couple of times on her way home, but now she was down and
wouldn't budge.

'Is she going to die?'

'Can you save her?'

'Why is she sleeping?'

'Do cows go to heaven?'

'Hm! What she needs is a pint of bitter!'

Now we got down to the task of sorting out her problem, as Griff
the butcher arrived with his usual quota of wisdom.

'Hey! Look!,' screamed a little brute as he peeped between the legs
of the Bobby. 'Flossie is passing red water!'

Sure enough. Her urine was a deep port wine red.

I beckoned to John, my student who was a city lad, to check her
carefully for any parasites. He produced several ticks which he
removed from underneath her neck.

'Do they have anything to do with it?'

John knew very little about cows at this stage but he was glad to
have an opportunity to show off his book knowledge of the subject and
really poured it on for his captive audience. While I prepared the

medication, he explained that the ticks carry a parasite which destroys the red blood cells, causing an acute anemia and, of course, the red urine. The lack of blood puts a strain on the heart—and so, Flossie found herself helpless on the town square.

We gave her an injection, deep into the muscle, high on her back leg, while the kids gaped with their mouths wide open. There was another scrimmage to get a better vantage point and some more of the young rascals felt the solid hand of the Bobby across their ears.

Amidst the commotion, Flossie raised her head, perked up her ears and staggered to her feet. She wobbled across the square for a few yards and suddenly fell over. Oh my! What a sight! She was having a heart attack! Unfortunately, that sometimes followed this injection. If only she could survive this ordeal, it was almost a certain cure. She fell over on to her side and every muscle in her body was twitching. Her eyes were rolling and her mouth was a sea of foam.

I tore into my magic bag and soon had some adrenalin trickling into her jugular vein. This was the recognized antidote—would it work?

There was deathly silence. I died a thousand deaths! Was she really

The Grist: *photo by W.D. Evans, St. Clears.*

going to let us down in front of all this crowd? The Vicar leaned forward and, putting his hand on my shoulder, he whispered, 'The darkest hour is the hour nearest the dawn. Keep the faith.' Flossie must have heard him, for soon the shaking stopped. Her eyes became steady, the foaming stopped. She raised her head, sat up and panted away while the sweat came pouring out all over her body—and mine! Flossie swished her tail and soon there she was, staggering to her feet! Away she went, straight for home—to the deafening roar of her huge gallery of cheerleaders.

John and I sighed with relief. We gathered our equipment and drove down to the beach. It was time for a breather.

We strolled along between the rocks and reflected on the drama of the town square. What if old Flossie had died? I was comforted by the knowledge that at least I would not have had to face a malpractice suit. Such an act was classified as being downright immoral and unethical.

Barnyard Surgery

'Mr. Griffiths, your cow has swallowed a piece of wire, a nail, or something. It is penetrating the wall of her second stomach and probably pushing towards her heart.'

'Oh, dear, my favourite cow. She's a good 'un—gave a pail-ful of milk every day until yesterday morning. John Davies had one like this a few years ago and her heart drowned in water.'

'That's what happens if you leave them alone.'

'What do you mean—what else can we do?'

'Ah! I think we can fix her for you. We will operate.'

'Operation!' exclaimed Davy Griffiths, as he leaned against the cowshed door, removing his dust-covered, well-ventilated hat and scratching his forehead.

'That's right,' I replied. 'We can open her up and take out the problem.'

'You, all on your own!'

'Of course, but I will ask my partner to work with me.' This was a new venture so I wanted to play it safe.

'Can't we wait to see how she will be in a day or so?'

'I suppose we could, but that would be taking a great risk and then it might be too late, like John Davies's cow.'

I took out my pencil and proceeded to explain the situation to my client, who had now been joined by his wife, Anna. I drew an outline of the cow's four stomachs and their close proximity to the heart on the wall which was white washed and made a pretty good 'blackboard.'

'Have you done any of these before?'

'Yes sir, one case—but she died because the operation was too late. I saw several of these operations in college.'

One of the most fascinating aspects of veterinary practice occurs when one has to try to convince a client that a certain line of treatment is indicated and should turn out to be successful. This kind of situation calls for unique diplomacy, especially when an elderly farmer's pet cow, bull, or horse is involved. Farmers are the most genuine people on earth. I was particularly blessed to have practised in an area which is recognized for the high standard of stockmanship. They know each animal by name and since the farms were small, very few over 100 acres, the livestock got almost individual attention. It was thus a matter of great concern when any of them became ill, especially one of the milk cows. The farmer lived off the produce of his land and even though few became rich, they lived a good life and raised their children to be fine, honest, hard working individuals.

Surgery on the farm was almost unknown in those days. This was due to the Animals Anaesthetics Act which had been previously in force in Britain. Under this Act, every major surgical operation required a general anaesthetic. Cattle are not very good subjects for general anaesthesia under the best of conditions. When such an animal is placed on her side, as during general anaesthesia, the stomach entrance to the gullet or food pipe is blocked. Gases accumulate in the stomach, causing the cow to bloat. This puts pressure on the diaphragm and the animal may die. Besides, under deep anaesthesia, relaxation of the muscles at the stomach entrance causes food to flow into the food pipe and may be inhaled into the lungs.

In those days chloroform or ether given by mask over the nostrils or chloral hydrate given in the vein or by a drench were the only anaesthetics available but none could be considered safe or satisfactory.

Following the repeal of this Act, a great new era in farmyard surgery began. I was privileged to be a member of the new young surgeons who helped it on its way.

'I will ask my senior partner to take a look at her. We will be back shortly.'

As we drove out of the farm yard, John, my young veterinary student, was very excited. 'Am I really going to be in on this?'

'Of course, might as well get your feet wet right away!'

'Why did you tell him that you wanted a second opinion?'

'Well, young man, that is where client psychology comes in—and don't you ever forget it! You see, I have only been out of college a short while and it takes time to build up a good reputation. Besides, my suggestion for surgery obviously hit the old boy rather hard. The operation is a new one, so naturally he wants to be pretty sure that our diagnosis is correct before he gives us the go ahead.'

'How do you diagnose these cases—just by examining the animal?'

'Glad you asked that! Let's see, you are now a second year student. You have learned a lot about biochemistry, physiology, anatomy, etc. Very soon you will be studying clinical diseases—that's when the fun of learning really starts. However, it is quite amazing how many fail to put their basic knowledge to practical use. This particular case is one in question.'

'I noticed that for quite a long time you stood back and just stared at the poor creature.'

'Good, now I can see you are on the right track already. I was not just admiring her fine conformation or sympathising with her predicament. I was doing something that you must develop if you want to become a successful practitioner—employing what I call 20/20 clinical vision.'

'What on earth is that? Do I need to have my eyes tested?'

'Heck, no! I mean you must learn how to observe an animal and be able to pick up clinical signs. But, first of all, you must be able to understand the *normal* animal.'

'Well, I think I know my anatomy and physiology pretty well. I passed my exams easily.'

'Great, but I wonder how well you can apply your knowledge?'

As we drove home up hill and down dale in the beautiful countryside, we had a wonderful discussion on clinical veterinary medicine. Will Rogers had once said, '*Personally, the cleverest doctor is the vet because his patient can't tell him what's wrong, he just has to know.*' Well, this is only partly true. Animals do have their sign language.

I reminded my student that a cow has four stomachs—two on the left and two on the right side of the abdomen. The first stomach is very large with a capacity of about thirty gallons. This is where the gases are produced. The second stomach is comparatively very small and lies between the first stomach and the diaphragm. The two stomachs contract in unison at regular intervals.

A cow takes food into the mouth in a different way from other farm animals such as the horse, sheep or pig. The cow pushes out her tongue and wraps it around some hay, grass or whatever the food, then scoops it into her mouth and swallows it. (Later the food is returned in small amounts to be chewed thoroughly—this is known as chewing the cud). If a foreign object such as pieces of wire or nails etc., happen to get into the feed or onto the grass, it will be swallowed along with the food and will drop into the second stomach. When this stomach contracts, any sharp object is pushed usually through the front wall, which is separated from the heart only by the diaphragm, a distance of a few inches.

'John, when we go back with Mr. Morgan, you check this cow carefully. Notice how she stands with her back arched, is reluctant to move, and every once in a while she will grunt—a short, stabbing kind of grunt. You will also observe that these grunts occur when her second stomach moves (or contracts).'

'How do I tell that?'

'Well, just observe her left side, behind the ribs. The first stomach lies under this area and you can see it moving up and down under the skin and muscles.'

'Now, recall your physiology and you will remember that these two stomachs work in unison, as it were—so, naturally, if there is a piece of wire penetrating the wall of the stomach (having been pushed through the stomach wall when it contracts), the cow will show pain and does this by grunting.'

'Now I know cows can talk,' John remarked.

'That's right, but also remember this—what I have told you about this cow is also true of other species of animals but in different ways. The cow is probably the best teaching model we have in this respect. I don't care whether you plan to become a small animal practitioner or an equine specialist, you develop your powers of observation and how to interpret the *normal* animal, then you can adapt your knowledge to any species.'

'I can't wait to get out of college—practice already seems to be such a great challenge.'

'Bob,' that's what his friends called him, 'Davy Griffiths at Cwmburla Farm has just the case we have been looking for.'

'What is it?'

'Wire in the stomach.'

'Really?'

'Yes! but I want you to take a look at her.'

Late that evening, the phone rang. Another emergency, I thought.

'I think you are nuts,' said my partner on the other end of the line. My heart sank to my feet (it didn't have far to travel!). After what appeared to be a long ordeal of silence, I could hear him chuckling, 'Are you still there?'

'Yes,' I whispered faintly.

'Okay,' he laughed. 'Yes, I agree with your diagnosis. I have arranged for us to operate tomorrow morning.' Tomorrow was going to be some day!!

The scene in Davy Griffiths' cowshed the next morning was a mixture of comic opera and exciting drama. The word had spread throughout the neighbourhood with lightning speed that a big operation was to take place and, since the farm was near a village, we were greeted by a gallery when we arrived—the policeman, baker, preacher, kids of all descriptions, and many neighbouring farmers—all wanting to help.

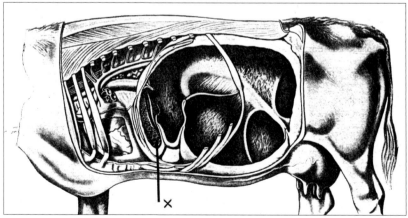

The second stomach with honeycomb lining (x) lies against the diaphragm which separates it from the heart. The first stomach occupies the rest of the abdominal cavity on the left side. (*After Nickel and Wilkens, 1955.*)

Our patient was tied to her stall in the middle of the cowshed. Every door and window was full of eager faces. Several climbed the beams and had good vantage points. Even the farm dogs sensed the great occasion. There was complete confusion when Fido, the nifty Welsh terrier chased a massive brown rat right across the cowshed in between the legs of anyone who stood in the way, just before the operation started!

Finally, the great event was underway. John, the student had shaved and disinfected the area of the skin over the cow's first stomach, on the left side behind the ribs. John Hughes, the farm hand, restrained the patient by placing his fingers in her nostrils while Jones, the Postman, held her tail straight up in the air to stop her kicking, whilst I injected local anaesthetic into the operation site. The surgical instruments were neatly laid on a tray perched on a 'table' made of three bales of straw.

A neat incision was made in the skin. The excited mutterings of the large audience gave way to deathly silence—except for the chickens cackling out in the yard—as the operation proceeded. Gracefully, we cut through the muscles as John handed the instruments as requested. Now we had reached the pale, greyish white stomach which rolled slowly back and fore as we opened up the abdomen. Soon, the stomach was opened. I wish I could really portray the tense moments for all of us as the surgeon inserted his arm into the first stomach and pushed steadily towards the second stomach.

Suddenly, the patient winced slightly—the surgeon removed his arm and triumphantly held up for all to see, the source of the poor cow's problem—a five inch piece of wire! Immediately there was great excitement and loud applause. The tension was gone. The drama had been lived and the whole barn was shrieking with laughter, joy, and shouts of 'Good boys, well done!' There is no feeling in the world to match the satisfaction of such an occasion.

'Where did she get this wire?' was the inevitable question.

'Let me see it,' remarked the proud owner. 'It's a piece of wire used to bale hay.'

'Fancy that! I wouldn't believe it possible,' said the preacher. We explained to them how a cow takes in food and how John Davies's animal had developed pericarditis.

We patiently sutured the stomach, muscles, and skin. To the amazement of the gallery, the cow did not seem to mind—she even chewed her cud long before the operation was over.

Davy Griffiths's Shorthorn cow survived her ordeal and became a celebrity in the neighbourhood, the topic of conversation in pubs, grocery shops, and no doubt a theme for a Sunday sermon!

There have been many occasions like this one but not always with a happy ending. Some operations were done too late, to the dismay of all concerned. Baling wire was replaced by binder twine and the incidence of these cases dropped dramatically.

I met Davy Griffiths at the local market one afternoon and there, dangling from his waistcoat watch chain like a solid silver heirloom, was a highly polished piece of baling wire!

There were other cases where nails, bolts, screws, and even parts of umbrellas were recovered! On one memorable occasion, I found a ladies' hair clip. The farmer's wife was standing by and, on examining the object, declared with utter anger, 'This is not one of mine!' Her young spouse had a lot to answer for that evening!

Since major operations could now be done under local anaesthesia, we were soon performing Caesarean sections and other major operations, such as for intestinal problems, with great success. The availability of penicillin and later, other antibiotics, was a major supporting factor. Our fee for major surgery was £5.

Early One Sunday Morning

Ting a ling! Ting a ling! Ting a ling!

I reached for the clock and turned off the alarm. I was deep in slumberland. The clock fell over with a thud which woke Mary enough to give me a good nudge in the ribs.

'Answer the phone.'

'Uh! I just turned it off.'

'I mean the telephone. Can't you hear it ringing?'

It was five thirty on a Sunday morning and my noise tolerance was at its deepest level in my biological cycle. It's always harder to wake up at this time of night—or morning!

'Hello.'

The 'tornado' at the other end was enough to wake the dead.

'Get up, you lazy devil. One of these days you will rot in bed!' bellowed old Jim Ludwick at the other end.

'Yh! What's the matter?'

'What's the matter indeed. Come on out here right quick,' he growled. 'Buttercup is choking to death!'

I crawled out of my bed, pulled on my night-call attire—riding breeches and a green pullover—and slid quietly downstairs. I was pulling up my Wellington boots when in crept Billy Neall, bleary eyed and looking rather sleepish! He was a tall, strapping ball-faced country lad, a third year veterinary student who was my understudy at the time. The night before—well, earlier that evening—when we finished our round of calls at about 9 p.m., Billy took a quick bath and went off on his favourite past time—chasing the farmers' daughters! But lately, he had been going rather steadily with the preacher's daughter, a beautiful blonde with a gorgeous schoolgirl complexion, destined to be a model. Billy had been staying with us for several weeks. We always regarded our students as part of the family, and my wife relished in teasing them about their most recent dates as well as matching them up with the eligible local princesses.

'Don't you ever go to bed? You will rot on your feet if you don't get more sleep. Better get your boots; we are going on a call.'

We got in my old Wolseley car, but it wouldn't start. The battery was low again.

Billy had to get out and push. The car free-wheeled down the street and when I finally slapped her into gear, the old tub let off a thunderous bang. Away we drove—no doubt having rudely awakened half the village! At least they would be awake in time for early church.

As usual at this unearthly hour, our destination was the other end of the practice.

As we tore up hill and cruised down dale, I recalled my own courting days. I finished my college career towards the end of World War II and petrol rationing was still strictly enforced. There was an adequate supply for farmers and vets, but the local Bobby kept a careful look-out for those not legally eligible to drive their cars. I was still single but had dated a farmer's daughter up the valley for some time. The biggest problem was that I had no means of transportation. Most of the time I was able to arrange my last round of calls in that part of the practice on Saturday nights, and there was many an occasion when I didn't arrive until almost midnight. My future mother-in-law was a very dear lady, but I wonder how many times she was tempted to chase me off her farm with the kitchen broom at those unbecoming hours.

One Saturday evening my date graciously consented to take the bus into town, and we went to the cinema. My hired bicycle (which belonged to my partner's wife) was out of action so I had permission to take the practice car. When we reached the village at the foot of the hill leading to her home, there was the local Bobby! He flashed his torch and we pulled up. Oh boy, was I in trouble! A quick safety inspection of my chariot would have resulted in me and my car being locked up! No tail light, hardly any brakes and many other deficiencies. He stooped over, looked into the car and recognized young Mary.

'Oh, I see you've been to town to fetch the vet.'

I coughed, she grimaced, and so did he!

'You better get to that sick cow. Good night!' And away we raced up the hill.

I rode my bicycle on many Saturday evenings after that escape. In the meantime, Billy had been catching up with some of his lost sleep, until we reached the steep, rugged hill with hairpin bends leading to Ludwig's farm. About half way up the hill to the farm our car stopped. The wheels had been spinning rather ominously as I tried to edge her up the steep slope. Now she could go no further. We reversed several yards and tried again, but it was no use. We could have walked, but we needed our equipment.

I am probably one of the least mechanically-gifted vets in creation, but I had long adopted the maxim, nothing ventured, nothing gained. There was nothing else to do but reverse to the bottom of the hill. Here, I turned the car around and engaged our obstacle course with a furious roar—in reverse! Dawn was now breaking, and I could see the road fairly well.

The little car responded magnificently and soon we were storming into the farm yard where old Ludwig was standing, leaning on his stick. He could hardly believe his eyes!

'Did you drive like that all the way? Have you been out on the town, or something?'

Jim Ludwig was a cattle dealer. His neighbours reckoned that the old rascal could buy something from a Jew and sell it to a Scotsman for profit! There he was with his usual 'pork-pie' hat flat on his head, a red handkerchief with white spots around his neck and wearing a ragged old tweed suit. He was an old bachelor who had earned the nickname of 'the parish stallion' because of his escapades with some of the eligible, and not so eligible, females in the county. He had sown his wild oats on some pretty fertile soil!

The case in question was a typical creature found among his livestock. He had bought the old red cow for a song in the local market and was hoping to make a quid or two on her. There she stood at the edge of the manure heap in the corner of the yard. A quick glance showed that she was in obvious distress as she coughed, spluttered and drooled large pools of saliva. The old boy told us that she had broken into the shed where he kept his newly gathered crop of potatoes. We managed to drive her into the cowshed and soon found that a potato had stuck in her throat. More precisely, it was lodged in her food pipe half way down her neck, a common site for an obstruction in cows.

While old Jim and Billy held her steady, I tried to work it back into her mouth. The old cow bellowed and tossed about like a tiger, falling in a heap in the feed trough with old Jim under her! The old boy's eyes were bulging like a couple of beacons. I had a horrible thought. He was suffocating to death, and my patient probably had a broken neck! I was greatly relieved when he bawled out in unprintable Welsh the biggest cursing I had ever received!

'Get the _____ off my chest. Do something!'

Billy and I grabbed her long horns and with a mighty heave we managed to pull the old cow out of his way. She was now a sorry sight, and something had to be done in a hurry! Bill fetched the chloral hydrate solution from the car and we slowly dripped about half an ounce into her jugular vein. Soon she appeared sleepy. I massaged her neck over the stuck potato, and to my relief it spun down the food pipe to her stomach. Saved again! We had given her just enough chloral to relax the muscles of her food pipe to relieve the obstruction.

Billy pulled our distraught client out of the manger and rescued his 'pork-pie' from the manure. The old boy was badly shaken and growled at both of us. Eventually, he settled down.

'I suppose I better thank you. I can't pay you now because I never write cheques on Sundays. Send me the bill.'

'That's alright.'

We gathered our equipment and we were soon on our way down to the valley. The autumn sun shone gloriously through the pine trees, and the meadows below were lined with all the beauty of the season.

Billy remarked that old Ludwig would not let Sunday stand in his way if there was a quick bargain likely to be pulled off!

We dropped in at the next village to check on any calls that may be waiting.

We were at the far end of our practice, and I had an understanding with old Dan Jones that my wife could always call in any messages for us in the neighbourhood. Dan was the proud proprietor of Waterloo House, an elegant name for the Trelech village grocery, petrol station and sundry goods of all descriptions. We came in through the back door. The shop was closed and Dan was lacing his shiny black Sunday boots when we arrived.

'There's a call for you to go to Pen Castell. They have a very sick sheep. My daughter has a cup of tea ready for you.'

I have spent many happy times with Dan and his family who helped me enormously when I was building up the practice. He loved to expound his views on anything from World War I to modern delinquency.

I had noticed that young Billy was rather restless and that something was really bothering him. Finally he chirped, 'Do you think we will be long on this call?'

'It all depends on what's wrong. Why?'

He fidgeted with his tie and unloaded his problem.

'Well,' he remarked in his Pembrokeshire drawl, 'I promised my girl that I would go to chapel with her this morning. They are holding their anniversary services.'

'Hm. I am afraid you've had it for this morning. That's how it is in this profession. You must attend when emergencies arise. Besides, my lad, true love never runs smoothly and Janice had better get broken in right now! You can phone her when we get to the farm.'

So poor Billy had his first taste of life in a rural practice. He was tired, hungry, and very love-sick. No doubt he felt that this belle would never look at him again for letting her down. After all, many a young lad had eyes on her!

Davy Morris had stayed home from chapel to tend to his sick Suffolk ram which was lying in a paddock behind the barn. He was in very bad shape, and his owner was full of anxiety. The young ram had won the Champion Cup at the local show only a month before. Now he was thin, his ears drooped and he breathed heavily. After some persuasion he got up.

'Isn't there a swelling under his jaw?' enquired Billy who had returned from his phone call.

'Good observation. Now why don't you take on this case and see if you can make a diagnosis.' After all, he needed something to get his mind off Janice!

Bill checked the ram's temperature and listened carefully with his stethoscope over the patient's chest. The ram had walked a few steps but could go no further. His heart was beating loud and fast. His gums and the inside of his eyelids were deathly white. I mean the ram's! The swelling under his jaw was soft and it was obviously an oedema or dropsy.

'Well, Bill, what do you make of him?' exclaimed the anxious client. 'He looks to me like a case of liver fluke.' Bill had a barrage of questions for the owner. He had kept his flock in a couple of fields with a stream running alongside one of them. A lot of the water was also stagnating around certain areas, and it had been a very wet summer.

Davy remarked that several of the ewes were not doing so well either. It was now late October. They obviously had picked up the parasites from the wet land in early summer along with the luscious grass. From the stomach they passed on to the intestine and finally found their way to the liver which is the 'factory' of the human or animal body.

The flukes were now messing up his whole system, and the ram was very anaemic.

'Well, Mr. Morris, we will have to give him a capsule of carbon tetrachloride—fluke medication.'

'Is that a cure?'

'I hope so, but he is in very bad shape as you can see. Better the day, better the cure, maybe.'

Billy brought out the capsules and pushed one down the ram's throat.

'Now let's check the others. Maybe they need some also.'

On our way to the meadow Davy related the tale about his neighbour whose prize bullock was given one of these pills to prevent fluke. In a matter of hours he was dead.

'Will that happen to my ram?'

'No. It is rather odd that the drug is very safe for sheep, but the same dose may kill a fat beef animal. Even more confusing is that a thin beast can tolerate it better than a fat one.'

The old man laughed heartily for he was rather a rotund little fellow. 'Then I better not take one!'

The fluke had affected nearly all the flock, but none was in serious condition. Davy and his men would round them up in the morning and treat them. We also advised him to drain the wet area around the streams where snails gather and act as intermediate hosts for the fluke parasite.

When we got back to the farmyard, Davy's wife was standing in the kitchen door.

'Come and join us for Sunday dinner.'

'Yes, yes, come on,' said Davy. 'So long as you take us as we are.'

'Thank you. That's nice of you.' Billy couldn't control his feelings. 'We haven't even had breakfast.'

'Right, and why don't you ask him how much sleep he had last night?'

At this time, through the barn gateway came the family Vauxhall. Our client's daughters were coming home from chapel.

Mrs. Morris was a gracious hostess, and we were soon enjoying a sumptuous farmhouse feast—roast beef, Yorkshire pudding, roast potatoes, french beans, cauliflower and then, home-made blackberry pie and custard—the traditional Sunday dinner.

Billy was really on cloud nine for what more could he had wished for than this wonderful meal, and across the table sat three absolutely breathtaking farmer's daughters in their very best Sunday dresses. I have to admit that I enjoyed the scenery also, for there is nothing so refreshing as country girls with beautiful schoolgirl complexions. First there was Heulwen (which is Welsh for 'Sunshine'), a lovely fourteen-year-old brunette but a little plump, probably puppy fat. At the other end was Eirwen (Snowdrop), a dazzling blue-eyed ten-year-old with a most delightfully catchy giggle, and in the middle was Bethan, a real heart-throb if ever there was—a tall rosy cheeked, eighteen year old brunette with absolutely gorgeous brown eyes. If ever there was a budding Miss World, it was Bethan, but like so many young damsels in the hills and valleys in those days, somehow they were never discovered.

'. . . *full many a flower is born to blush unseen . . .*'

The Greedy Cow

Emily and her husband, Will, lived on a small acreage close to town. Will was employed by the County Council and Emily spent her time looking after Will, three cows, and a lot of chickens. She was the kindest old soul, rather large, with a hearty laugh, but she had a temper and chased many a neighbouring kid with the kitchen broom—and demanded instant veterinary service whenever she called.

'Are you there,' came the familiar, high-pitched voice across the telephone. 'Come quick! Bertha is very sick! I think she has milk fever!'

'When did she calve?'

'Oh, several weeks ago. Come on out here, quick!'

'All right. I am on my way.'

I had known Emily for several years and understood her ways—most of the time! Her 'emergencies' were not always that urgent.

At that time I had a student, Malcolm, 'seeing practice' with me. He and I climbed into our rickety Ford 8 practice vehicle and sped to Emily's farm.

There she was, kneeling over poor Bertha, a rather well-cared for eight year old Jersey cow. Bertha was stretched out and showed very little sign of life. Her horns and ears were cold, her pulse was fast and weak and her breathing was rather shallow and rapid. She had a very obvious diarrhoea.

'Well, Malcolm, what do you think?' I said. Being an astute, young man anxious to learn, he came up with some ideas.

'What about milk fever?' he asked, since she was a pretty good dairy cow that produced a lot of milk.

'I doubt it—she calved several weeks ago,' I mused.

'But that does not rule it out,' he insisted.

'Right, Malcolm, and don't you ever forget that—and if in doubt, you better give a calcium injection in the vein—but there are signs here which lead to another possibility. Can you detect them?'

'Well, she is stretched out under a tree. What about lightning strike?'

'Can you see any burning marks anywhere on the hair?'

'No, and besides, we have not had any thunderstorms lately.'

I chuckled, for I had a client who always insisted that there had been a thunderstorm over his farm every time an animal died out in the fields!

'What else do you notice?' This was an essential part of his professional training. 'Tell me what you can see or feel. Then we can work out a possible diagnosis.'

It is essential for a young, budding vet to understand the importance of such a procedure. It can save him a lot of embarrassing moments by otherwise jumping to conclusions too soon.

'The pulse is fast. The opposite is the case in milk fever.'

'Good observation.'

'What about this diarrhoea? That is not a sign commonly observed with milk fever.'

'That is right. They are usually constipated.'

During this time I was preparing a battery of questions for our friend, Emily—if I could get a word in somewhere because she was very excited and insisted on a quick diagnosis and cure.

'Now, Mrs. Jones, tell me something—what have you been feeding her lately?'

'Nothing unusual—grass, some cattle cake—that's all'.

'Did you notice anything wrong with her yesterday or the day before?'

'Not really—oh, yes. She was rather bloated on one side and was a little wobbly as she walked. Her milk yield was down a lot.'

'Now, Malcolm, what does that tell you?'

'Has she been into the apple orchard?' he inquired.

'No way,' said Emily. 'I only have two trees and no apples this year!'

'I notice you have a lot of chickens. Where do you keep their feed?'

'In a shed next to the cow shed.'

'Have you checked there today?'

'Not yet.'

We walked across to the shed and noticed that the latch was broken and the door was slightly open. Inside there was a large bin which stored the chicken feed—half empty.

'Here's our problem.' I remarked as I scooped a handful of the ground feed and gave it to my student. 'Overeating disease—that's it' Bertha was a pet cow and like many of her kind, had a habit of getting into everything. Since the door was unlatched, she found her way into the feed room and simply engorged herself with a banquet of chicken feed.

'But she is used to cattle feed,' remarked Malcolm. 'Why should this cause her trouble?'

'Well, she is only used to small amounts per feed and, besides, chicken feed is much more concentrated than what she eats.'

We finally convinced Emily that Bertha was in severe shock due to acidosis because of the after effects of overeating the feed. We gave her lots of fluids intravenously and propped her up.

The author dressed in the traditional winter attire for veterinarians (breeches and knee length stockings). Also pictured George Thomas, brother-in-law, centre, and Jack Williams.

'Malcolm, never forget this point. You must not let a ruminant lie on her side too long, otherwise, she will bloat because the gases cannot get out of her stomach.'

We passed a stomach tube and pumped in a bucketful of antacids and some medicine to soothe the lining of the gut along with more fluids because she was very dehydrated.

'Before we leave for our next call, there is one very important thing we have to do, ' I remarked.

'I know,' chirped in Malcolm, who was always alert after midday, 'We must check the other cows.'

They were both grazing heartily in a field behind the house. We gathered our equipment and, as usual, washed, cleaned, and disinfected our rubber overshoes.

Emily called from the house, 'Your tea is ready.' She had a very special kind of tea—there was usually something else in it on a cold day or special occasion.

As we were leaving, Emily gave me a dozen eggs for my wife.

We checked back the next morning and found our patient chewing her cud to her heart's content and Emily happy.

She Won't Hear the Cuckoo

The wretched animal was huddled on the straw bedding in the corner of the hayshed. The winter had been very hard and the harvest the previous summer had mostly been ruined by the wet weather. Hay was scarce and a lot of it was mouldy. Will Jenks was not exactly the smartest livestock man in the area. He spent most of his time in the neighbourhood pubs and his poor wife struggled hard to make ends meet to raise their son and two daughters. Will had a strange philosophy about paying his bills. At the beginning of each month, if he was sober—he would place all the bills in a pot and take out a few at random and hoped to pay them! However, any creditor who chided him for not paying up would not have *his* bill even included in the pot!

Will's cow had been down for a week. The rings on her horns said that she was at least eight years old and she was due to calve in a few weeks. To say the least she was rather thin!

Will's neighbour was a cheerful old soul and when he saw the car drive up the road, he had to come by to see what was going on.

'I don't like the looks of her—she won't hear the cuckoo, eh!?'

'What did he say?' remarked my student, Bill. The old boy hooted with laughter—and so did I!

'Haven't you heard that expression before?' I remarked.

'Well, tell me, what is it?'

'It means—will she pull through? In other words, what is the prognosis?' The cuckoo comes in April every year and this was early in March.

'Will she?'

'I doubt it!'

We proceeded to examine the poor creature. It has always been my custom to let my students try to make a tentative diagnosis on their own by a process of discussion of the possible causes, though I was always careful to avoid embarrassing them in front of clients (the 'chewing out' usually occurred on our way to the next call).

The 'downer cow' syndrome is undoubtedly the most frustrating of cases to deal with. There are so many possible causes, and besides, in many cases, no definite cause can be determined.

'What is the golden rule to be observed in these cases?' I enquired of my young understudy.

'Always check for a broken leg or pelvis.'

'Right—and don't you ever forget.' There have been many occasions when this simple procedure has been overlooked.

We checked and found her bones to be intact.

'Her eyes are sunk deep in their sockets.'

'Right—and we have a saying for that too—'When the eyes go in, the cow goes out!'—because of dehydration.'

We finished our examination and came up with a diagnosis.

'Agrociosis,' I proclaimed.

My audience stared at me in amazement.

'That's right, she is short on groceries! Or, if you prefer, how about this one; she has high trough disease—the trough is up here and she can't reach it and probably there is nothing much in it!'

'You mean, this cow has been starved almost to death.'

'Precisely,' I replied. But, it is hard to get clients to accept this kind of diagnosis.

Before we left the farm, the old boy leaned over the fence and remarked, 'Mr. Williams, you tell your young student that one bale of hay before Christmas is worth the whole load after the New Year'

'Good advice, Mr. Hughes. Good day!'

We drove away and held a lengthy discussion on the need for good nutrition. This animal had been starved and was so weak that she could not get up.

Will Jenks' cow was pushing up the daisies long before the cuckoo arrived. Next year he would feed his stock better—we hoped.

Not all 'downer cows' are like Will's cow. Ianto Hines had a cow that was down in the middle of the field. She was quite old, at least twelve years and in fair condition. A complete examination failed to reveal any broken bones or some possible disease. Ianto was a shrewd, philosophical fellow. He had lots of money but never spent any unless he really had to. His Shorthorn cow had been down for several days but every effort to get her up failed—even the old trick of placing the farm dog on her only caused her to shuffle her legs and bellow. I gave her a stimulant and returned the next day. She was still down and since my client did not want to spend more money on her and because she was barren we agreed to salvage her by sending her to the slaughterhouse. Ianto would probably get a few quid for her. However, when the lorry came to pick her up, apparently her ears perked up and the old girl struggled to her feet! Whew! And didn't that story spread around the neighbourhood and the local cattle market!

Meidrim Village. *Photo by W. D. Evans, St. Clears.*

Cwmbach Village with a typical farmhouse, buildings and hayshed in the background.

St. David's Day

Our morning round took us up the valley from St. Clears to Meidrim, a peaceful village at the foot of the hill that climbs towards Trelech.

My student was an attractive Scandinavian who had come over to stay with a friend who had married a local farmer's son. She was a veterinary student in Stockholm.

'Why are these children going to school dressed in those odd looking clothes?' she enquired in her delightful accent.

I chided her because I thought they looked beautiful.

'Don't you know today is a special day in Wales?'

'Is that why you are wearing that tie?'

'That's right. I'm glad you noticed it,' I remarked as I stroked my Welsh tie of solid green decorated with the red dragon of Wales.

'Don't you know the date today?'

'It's March the first.'

'Right—and it's St. David's Day. These girls are wearing their Welsh costumes—a tall, black, stove-topped hat, a shawl and a beautiful plaid skirt.'

'Who was St. David?'

'The Patron Saint of Wales, of course. England has St. George, Scotland has St. Andrew, and the Irish have St. Patrick. It's said in some history records that at one time, Wales had so many saints she gave St. Patrick to Ireland!'

'What do you mean?'

'Well, apparently his mother was a Welsh girl who married a Roman soldier. It seems that they were on a pilgrimage trip to Rome and somehow their young son ran away, tried to get back to Wales on his own, and landed in Ireland!'

'Let's get back to St. David.'

'He was a great Welshman and a pioneer of Christianity here. He is buried in St. David's Cathedral, which is down by the coast about thirty miles from here.'

'Why are they wearing daffodils?'

'That is the national emblem of Wales. Some wear a big leek—a kind of onion. My wife will have a beautiful bunch of daffodils on the dinner table tonight.'

'How do most people celebrate today?'

'The schoolchildren will probably have a concert with folk dancing to the harp and lots of singing. Tonight, there will be a concert, a banquet, or an *Eisteddfod.*'

'What on earth is that?'

'*Eisteddfod?* That's a great Welsh tradition. It's a contest—in music, verse, or drama. You should try and attend the one in our village tonight. If you really want to hear the true sound of music, that's the place to be. Wales is known all over the world as the Land of Song. Put three or four Welshmen together and they will soon form a choir!'

'I heard some good singing coming from the pub last night!'

'The competition among choirs in some of these *Eisteddfodau* is terrific! There will probably be so much competition in the various items on the programme tonight, you will be lucky to get home before breakfast!'

We stopped at the village to see Dai Pugh's Welsh pony. He had been lame for a few days and could hardly put his left foot on the ground.

'I think he has the thrush,' remarked the old boy as he led his three-legged pony out of the stable.

Kim held the horse's leg between her knees while I cleaned the mud off the foot.

'He certainly stinks,' protested my student as she tried to pinch her nose with one hand.

'That's one of the symptoms. It is caused by an infection between the clefts of the frog, the spongy part of the foot. But, you must always check very carefully in case a foreign body is lodged in there.'

Dai Pugh nodded his approval for he had been a breeder of Welsh ponies for many years.

We poured some medication into the frog and wrapped the foot.

'Now you must come inside to celebrate. My wife is getting things ready.'

We entered the tiny cottage near the bridge. Even the little stream was full of music on this auspicious day. Facing the kitchen door was an old Welsh dresser with blue plates and golden lustre jugs. Cured hams and sides of bacon hung from ceiling hooks at the other end. Myfanwy Pugh proudly displayed her Welsh lovespoon to our Swedish companion. It was a custom in the old days for the bride-to-be to receive one from her lover. I wonder if this was the origin of 'spooning'?

'I don't expect you are busy today, Mr. Williams,' enquired Dai Pugh. 'We have plenty to do. I don't expect the cows know it's St. David's Day !!'

'You must have a cup of tea and some Welsh cakes.'

'I haven't tasted these before. They are delicious. How do you make them?' enquired Kim in between bites of the sumptuous delicacy.

'Nothing to it,' remarked Myfanwy as she pointed to a round cast iron plank beside the open fireplace. 'You prepare a mix and add lots of raisins, then cook them on this plank.'

Kim had been thoroughly baptized into the Welsh way of life by the time we left for the next call. We climbed the hill to Pencribyn to start a tuberculin test of Twm Lloyd's mixture of dairy cows. Twm had forgotten that I had sent him a card the previous day so the cows were still in the field. Since it was not yet noon, I knew we were in for a run around.

Twm sent Meg, his Welsh Corgi, into the meadow to bring them home. Corgis are mostly kept nowadays as house pets but the breed was developed originally to round up cattle. Their low physical stature enabled them to race up behind the cows and snap them on their heels without being kicked. Lloyd's Corgi was the Pembrokeshire type with a short tail and stocky body. The Cardiganshire Corgi has a longer body and a very long tail.

The cattle were soon on their way through the yard gate and then the fun (or agony!) started. Obviously in this herd there must have been a couple with thoroughbred blood because as soon as we tried to drive them into the cowshed, they took off and cleared the yard fence like a bunch of antelopes! Kim leaped over the gate and took up the chase while the farmer and his servant tried to cut them off from going to the river. They were too late. The crazy beasts charged right into the water and finally came to a halt on a little island near the other side. No amount of cursing or splashing stones would make them budge. Finally, Twm Lloyd arrived on his Welsh cob and took off into the river after them.

This did the trick, and luckily, when they reached the river bank, they took off this time in the right direction—straight for the barn. We managed to get them inside and soon our morning's work was done.

'Dinner is ready,' came a voice from the kitchen door. Country folk have dinner at noon and supper in the evening.

We removed our Wellington boots and went into the house for another feast.

'Do you like *cawl*?' enquired our delightful hostess.

'You better had,' chirped in old Twm. 'That will make a woman out of you!' Kim had yet another cookery lesson.

Cawl is a Welsh soup of boiled bacon, leeks or onions, potatoes and vegetables.

That afternoon we had to work at double speed to catch up with the rest of the calls. My wife and children were getting ready for the *Eisteddfod* as we finally arrived home.

'Can I come with you to the *Eis*—-?—the festival?' enquired young Kim.

'Well, certainly, if you don't mind listening to Welsh all evening.'

'I don't mind. It's the singing I want to hear. That's a universal language, isn't it?'

A special day and a special guest called for a little celebration.

My wife poured the *Bristol Cream* and we drank a toast to St. David.

'*Iechyd da i bob Cymro*'—which means 'Good health to all Welshmen.'

'And the lovely Swede!—let's not forget our guest!'

While we relaxed over the sherry, our three red-headed children, Thomas, Michael and Betsi gave us a private audition, perched on a stool in the middle of the dining room. The *Eisteddfod* was a great success, well into the early morning hours.

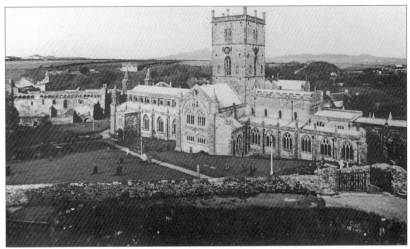

St. David's Cathedral.

Two farm girls dressed in Welsh costume.

Spring Time

Springtime brought out the wonders of nature which were always a joy to behold, even for those of us who sped along the familiar country lanes often at break-neck speed. I loved to listen to the cuckoo at the crack of dawn for here was the true harbinger of spring.

Practice at this time of year was always a mad rush with calls coming from all directions by day and by night. March was invariably miserable and it seemed the month would never run out. High winds, lashing rains, and on one occasion, over three feet of snow which stayed around for several weeks. This was unusual for the south-west, since most of the cold weather came from the east.

For several days we were completely snowbound. It was quite a change for my wife to have me around all day—and the children even became reacquainted with their father! The worst part of the snowstorm was that eventually the main roads were cleared but the rest were still impassable. As sure as day follows night, you can bet your boots that some creature, great or small, will decide to have a calf or some pups a long way from nowhere—usually in the middle of the night.

Such was the case with Haile Selassie's cow! My client earned his nickname because of his remarkable resemblance to the Emperor of Abyssinia (Ethiopia). He farmed with his brother and two sisters on a hill overlooking the sea.

I drove along the icy highway for about six miles and then took the minor road leading south. Half a mile further along I came to a dead end—the snow drifts completely blocked the way. Now for a long trek to the farm.

I will never be able to recall how many times I tumbled headlong in a drift or lost my Wellington boots along the way.

As I approached the final hill to my destination, the wind was blowing hard and I said good-bye forever to my favourite trilby hat which probably landed in the sea.

At last I saw a light in the distance which seemed at the time like a beacon in the pitch darkness. My client was coming to meet me with a Hurricane lamp.

We reached the barn where Daisy's uterus had turned inside out after calving. It was bulging behind her in the straw. I recalled that Sunday morning on Dad's farm when I had made up my mind to grow up like Morgan the Vet! He was my idol then and he should have shown me one like this—in the snow! The books didn't tell it like this either!

My client had everything ready and soon we were inside the kitchen having put Daisy comfortable for the rest of the night. His sister, Mary, was there to greet us.

'This will thaw your blood,' she remarked in her quiet Pembrokshire drawl, as she handed me a huge mug.

It was piping hot. I took a sip and immediately I thought my throat was on fire.

'How'd ya leik tha-t?' whispered old Willie as he took a huge gulp from his tankard.

'It's great! What is it?'

My hostess had introduced me to her brand new vintage of home-brewed beer.

'I thought I would heat it up for you and add a spoonful of sugar and some ginger. It will save you from the flu.'

'Are you sure it isn't dynamite?'

We spent the rest of the night by the coal fire under the huge open chimney in the kitchen. When daylight finally arrived, Willie drove me across the fields aboard his Fordson tractor back to my car.

When the snow finally cleared, the tempo of practice stepped up enormously. I was glad when my student arrived to see practice with me again during the Easter vacation. Springtime has always been hectic in country practice but this one was the limit. Day and night we struggled to keep up with all sorts of cases—calving, foaling, farrowing, milk fevers, cows unable to get up, mastitis—let alone the endless numbers of retained afterbirths.

One Wednesday afternoon in April, however, made all the rest of the cases seem ordinary routine calls. We were called to see John Morris's Jersey cow. John was a lorry driver for the local milk factory and he had left a note about his cow. His wife had complained that the milk for the past few days had a peculiar taste and that this Jersey cow's breath smelled like pear-drops. She had calved normally a week previously but she did not have her usual amount of milk and her appetite was poor.

'Huw, this is just the case we have been waiting for!' I remarked, keeping my eyes glued to our patient standing in the corner of the barn.

'She doesn't seem unusual to me.'

'Come over here. Now, do you notice something different? Just watch her carefully.'

'Well, she is pretty thin!'

'Can't you see that bulge just behind her last rib on her left side?'

He moved up and palpated the obvious swelling.

'It feels as if it is full of air or gas.'

'You're improving.'

'That's not her rumen (first stomach).'

'You are getting closer! What is it then?' I took out my stethoscope and placed it over the last ribs, in the middle. I flicked her ribs with my fingers and found the evidence I needed. I gave out a loud 'Hurrah' as my excitement took over.

'Place your stethoscope alongside mine and listen to the music!'

Huw had sensed the significance of the occasion and heard the same 'tinkling' sound.

For some time I had been on the look out for these cases which I had read about in *The Veterinary Record*.

John Morris came into the cowshed as I was about to explain the situation to my understudy.

'Well, John, this is a first of her kind,' I remarked as he leaned over the stall.

'What's that?'

'She has a displaced abomasum!' Quickly, I explained to him that a cow has four stomachs—two on the left and two on the right. For some reason, they sometimes get out of line! The bulge behind the ribs was her fourth stomach (the abomasum) which had found its way under the first stomach and was now jammed in on the left side.

'That's a serious problem, isn't it?'

'I hope not.' I had never seen one before but here was our chance to work on a 'miracle.'

We took our patient out to the orchard behind the kitchen, placed a rope in two loops around her body and pulled her to the ground. I instructed John to steady her head while Huw and I rolled her, first on to her back and then briskly over to one side.

'Now let her up and let's see what happens.'

The old cow soon got untangled from the rope and immediately put her head down to graze.

'That's more than she has eaten for a week,' remarked my client with his hair sticking on end!

Our adventure was obviously a success. The stomachs were back in place again.

This was the first of many of these cases that I encountered during the ensuing years. They did not all turn out to be as spectacular as this one for they had a tendency to recur. For these we had to perform surgery to replace the stomach and fix it on the right side.

We left our client in high spirits. Huw had a brand new one to record in his case-book for his finals. We had our usual seminar as we drove to our next call on the other side of the river.

'Now I know why it is so important to understand the normal animal first,' admitted young Huw as I prodded his brain with a series of questions.

'That's why we spent so much time listening to the 'stomach music' in Harry Lloyd's cows the other day.' He recalled that Harry was out in the field when we arrived at his farm recently, so while we waited for him, Huw and I took our stethoscopes and listened to the heart beats, lung sounds, and stomach movements of some of the normal cows in the barn.

'I would never have understood the meaning of that peculiar tinkling sound had it not been for the other lesson.'

Both of us had learned a lot from the case of the little Jersey cow with the twisted stomach.

St. Clears YFC Agricultural Show committee and judges (1948).

St. Clears Parish Council; late 1950s. *(Photo by W. D. Evans, St. Clears.)*

Easter Time

Easter time was probably the most enjoyable time of the year even though it was a particularly busy time in a country practice. This was the season of calving and foaling cases, and lots of ailments which seem to afflict animals following the ravages of winter.

Good Friday, being a national holiday, was usually devoted to church services for Anglicans and music festivals in most of the Welsh chapels or village halls. The festival or *Gymanfu Ganu* is a specifically Welsh function and the most heartwarming thrill in the world to me is to hear the melodious sound of a Welsh choir.

Easter Saturday was the most popular time of year for weddings. I have always had a flair for big occasions and weddings in Wales were usually great events. Only high society married in the afternoon. The rest of us had a morning wedding, usually about 11 o'clock. The wedding ceremony naturally had lots of music and hymn singing by the congregation. Very often most of the parish would turn out in force at the chapel. They were the unofficial guests or onlookers who would fill the gallery upstairs. The bride and bridegroom would leave from the 'big pew' at the front of the chapel for the vestry to sign the register of marriages, followed by the bridesmaids, best man, and the minister.

In the meantime, the well-wishers would line up outside the chapel while the invited guests stayed in their pews. The organist would strike up the Wedding March and soon the happy couple would return to the chapel and down the aisle to be greeted at the front door by little girls with silver horse shoes which they presented to the bride as a symbol of luck. The corridor of onlookers would shower the happy young couple with rice and confetti and they would finally get to their car decked with white ribbons for the journey to the reception.

Usually, they did not get very far!—for down the road would be a bunch of eager chldren who would hold a rope across the road and would not let them pass until the bridegroom had thrown out some money as 'ransom!' I well remember six different groups on the lane to the reception when we were married.

The reception is referred to as the wedding breakfast which is usually a sumptuous feast of the finest country cooking. The meal on most occasions is a sit-down affair held in the bride's home following weeks of careful preparation, but more recently, at a local hotel followed by a lavish party in the evening.

The highlight of the breakfast is the cutting of the wedding cake—a rich fruit cake with marzipan and Royal icing. The big moment arrives when the preacher or close friend of the family would propose a toast to the bride and bridegroom. The champagne would flow and the nervous bridegroom would follow with his maiden speech—'on behalf of my wife (Hurrah!!) and myself . . .'. His ordeal was over! He would propose a toast to the bridesmaids for whom the best man would reply. Then followed the reading of telegrams sent by well-wishers for the couple's happy future, such as 'May your troubles be little ones, and your little ones no trouble!'

I have known wedding receptions to continue for hours with speech after speech. Every uncle and friend seems to think it is a duty to perform on such an auspicious occasion. The young couple has other ideas!

Easter Sunday was practice as usual, for no matter what the occasion, the vet has to be on call *all* the time. Since I was the only one of our firm of vets located in this little town, I would take care of most of the weekend emergencies—at least those were only the cases we *wanted* to deal with but invariably there were others such as 'Mr. Williams, I was doing the Sunday round, looking at my stock and I found this old cow lying on her own in the corner of the field!' She had been sick for several days obviously. Or the usual tale, 'I can only get help on weekends—would you come out to castrate some pigs.'

In spite of such irritations, I always loved Easter. One delightful Easter Sunday started with an early morning call. Davy Hopkin's Holstein cow was stretched out in the field when he went to fetch his cows for the morning milking. I managed to get my bleary-eyed student, Andy, to shuffle out of bed and away we went with the usual high speed at the crack of dawn. Andy was a sharp young student from Cambridge who was seeing practice with me during his Easter vacation. We were met at the farm by the anxious farmer's wife who knew exactly what we needed for there had already been several cases of milk fever on this farm.

We went into the kitchen, poured the calcium borogluconate powder in a clean saucepan and added a half-pint of water. While our medicine was being sterilized on the kitchen stove, we chatted over the usual cup of tea. In those days medicines were not pre-packaged, and for years we prepared our milk fever solution in this way. It had one advantage in that injecting the warm solution seemed to produce quicker results.

'My son, Idris, will take you to the field,' chirped the hospitable lady. 'My husband is busy with the milking and we are hoping to get to chapel on time!'

We walked across the yard, over a stile and into *Parc Castell* (field). The old Friesian cow was lying helpless in the morning sun.

'She is dead!' exclaimed Idris. 'Oh my! Dad will be saying it !'

Andy knelt over the cow to examine her.

'Gosh, what do you think?'

I checked her eyes and noticed an occasional faint blink. Her respirations were so shallow and far apart that the animal really seemed to be dead.

'Andy, this is the kind of case a vet likes to see—especially if he is young and needs to build up his reputation.

'Why do you say that?'

'Give me a cow with milk fever that is almost on her last breath, and I can show you a 'miracle'.'

We took out the needle and attached it to a special type of rubber syringe and pumped the warm calcium solution into the milk vein under her belly.

'Mr. Vet, what is that stuff you're giving daddy's cow?' piped young Idris in his customary Welsh.

'We are giving her calcium.'

'What's that?'

'It's a mineral which every man and animal needs. This cow has a calcium deficiency.'

'Why is she sleeping?'

'That's a good observation, Idris. Now, Andy, you explain it to him.'

Andy was delighted to show off his wealth of knowledge on the subject because it was a question on one of his terminal exam papers just before Easter. He told young Idris all about it as the young lad looked up at him with his mouth wide open, his school cap perched at an acute angle and his weekend trousers hanging well below his knees.

'Look, she is waking up!' shouted young Idris, holding the seat of his trousers.

'That's right. The calcium is already working.' Andy had explained to him the effect of a lack of calcium on her nervous system.

Andy had placed his stethoscope inside the cow's left elbow several times since we started to give the injection.

'Why are you doing that?' enquired the curious kid.

'I am keeping a check on her heart beats. Sometimes when we give calcium, it causes the heart to flutter and the cow may die unless we are careful.'

'Oh! Can I have a try?'

Our patient was now breathing regularly and swished her tail several times. Soon she was sitting up and belched volumes of gas from her stomach.

'Now I know why cows must never be left on their side too long. Those gases collecting in her stomach could easily kill her.'

'I see you are well on your way to becoming a good vet, Andy.'

We gathered our equipment and strolled towards the farm house.

'Look, look, look, she is on her feet,' gasped Idris as he looked back over the stile.

The young boy raced to the house to finish his Easter egg. Boy, did he have a tale for his Sunday School class!

'Marvellous!'

'Thank you, once again for coming out on Easter Sunday,' remarked Mrs. Hopkins as she pressed a bunch of daffodils into my hand.

'*Diolch yn fawr*,' I replied.

As we climbed into the car, Andy grinned broadly.

'What did you tell her?'

'Diolch yn fawr'—that's Welsh for 'Thank you very much'. He was to learn a lot of phrases in the coming weeks.

When we reached the end of the farm lane, we pulled up and left the car.

'Springtime is really marvellous, isn't it?' gasped my young colleague as we stood on the hedge looking down over the valley. To our left was a small forest and the trees were already alive again, bathed by a carpet of crocus, daffodils, and bluebells. Right below us, the beautiful green fields were a marvellous playground for the spring crop of lambs.

A lovely poem which I had learned in Whitland Grammar School came to my mind. Perhaps I should say, one of many the we *had* to learn for Miss Bobs, our very strict English teacher—pages and pages of poetry by Keats, Shelley, Wordsworth, let alone endless lines from *Julius Caesar*. I hated it then, but now I am already eternally grateful to her for the academic enrichment. This poem 'The Autobiography of a Super Tramp' was by J. H. Davies.

'What is this life if full of care
We have no time to stand and stare

No time to see when woods we pass
Where squirrels hide their nuts in grass

No time to stand beneath the boughs
And stare as long as sheep or cows

A poor life, this, if full of care
To have no time to stand and stare.'

Down in the valley, the chimneys of white-washed cottages in the little village could barely be seen through the morning mist. The silence was almost astounding. All of a sudden, from the forest came the true signal of springtime. A cuckoo perched high on a limb, poured forth her greeting to the morning sun. You can travel all over the world but there is nothing to compare with the melodious sound of the cuckoo on a sunny spring morning.

The cuckoo fluttered away to another part of the wood. High above us, the skylark, the 'ethereal minstrel, pilgrim of the sky,' climbed towards the heavens, while down in the valley the curlew joined the delightful chorus.

We drove down into the valley and admired the little girls in their gorgeous Easter bonnets as they climbed the steps of the local chapel. We called in to check on the progress of a couple of patients on the other side of the valley. We were about to move off again when Andy signalled.

'Can you hear that singing?'

I stopped and smiled with delight.

'Yes, Andy, there is one sound even better than the cuckoo!'

'What's that?'

'Welsh hymn singing. Just listen!'

'I expect it is even better on Easter morning.'

'Why?'

'All those C&E's are there.'

'Who are they?'

'The Christmas and Easter crowd!'

All we needed to make it a perfect morning was a good Sunday lunch. We could hardly wait. Yes! My wife had it all ready—Easter lamb, green peas, new potatoes, and mint sauce! Mmm! Mmm!

It was indeed a Happy Easter.

Shire horses at the Royal Welsh Show, 1979.
(*Photo by Dr. Edward Sterner, Ionia, Michigan.*)

Trelech farmers.

Sir Toli the Third

Bill's eyes were as red as the rising sun as he dragged himself into the Morris before we drove off on yet another emergency call.

'Been out on the town again?' I remarked as he finished lacing his shoes.

'No. Remember we gave Olwen Evans a ride into town the other day? I took her out last night.'

'Oh, how is Sir Toli getting along?' I needn't have asked about Olwen, because she was always full of the joys of spring.

'Olwen thinks he is doing fine.'

'Phew! That's a relief—he got rather close to the Jordan' (almost died).

'Yes, Olwen told me the full story. Did you know that you were the third vet to be called in, let alone the local quack?'

'I had a hunch. After all, it was pretty obvious that he had been sick for quite a while when I first saw him. He was so thin you could hang your trilby hat on his hips.

Sir Toli the Third was Daniel Evans' famous Shire stallion. I remember his sire, Sir Toli the Second, very well. It was during my elementary school days at Llangynin. Every Spring, Dan would lead him around from farm to farm in the parish during the breeding season. It was the highlight of our school week when one of the kids would cry out, 'Hurray, Sir Toli is coming!'

Like a swarm of bees, all of us would abandon our game of soccer during the lunch hour and climb on top of the school wall alongside the road leading through the village.

Dan was quite a showman—and so was his stallion. As they approached the school, Dan would tap him briskly across the ribs. Sir Toli would immediately break into a trot and lift his heavily feathered legs majestically. His tail was neatly interwoven with a red, white and blue ribbon and the top of his mane was also decked up. He was our parish idol—and he had quite a gang of cheerleaders. The more we cheered, the more he showed off.

Dan was a real character who loved a glass or more of whisky. One day he was walking Sir Toli on the road having visited a few farms where he had been offered his favourite *nogin*. As he approached the next village the local Bobby stopped him for being drunk in charge of a horse! Old Dan was a wily soul—in his quiet inimitable way he handed the policeman the reins and spluttered, 'Well then, you lead him!'

Sir Toli the Second died from grass sickness. It was a sad day in the neighbourhood when that happened.

'Mr. Williams, my calf has gone nuts,' exclaimed old Delwyn Prydderch as he led us to the little whitewashed barn in the corner of the yard. As I leaned over the barn door I found five well-fed Friesian heifer calves about four weeks old. One was standing in the corner with her front legs wide apart. Thick foam drooled from her mouth as she kept grinding her teeth all the time. Suddenly she appeared to go crazy—she started bolting around the pen and even tried to climb the wall.

'This animal is as blind as a bat,' remarked Bill as he took off after her and tried to bring her under control, but she was more than he could handle. She fell over and went into convulsions.

'What do you feed these calves, Delwyn?' I enquired as I moved over to inspect the wooden partition.

'They are on milk twice a day, and a little grain mixture free choice.'

'Well, that rules out milk staggers.'

'What would that be?'

'It's a metabolic upset due to a lack of magnesium in the blood of calves fed only milk for several weeks.'

'I read in the books about rabies. Don't they go into fits with that?'

'Yes, they do sometimes, but you don't have to worry about that here. We don't have any on this island, thank goodness. I saw a case while I was staying with a vet in France last year, though.'

I was not in a hurry to disrupt our patient, because I knew the fit would pass off and the calf would appear to be normal again. Besides, I had my eye on the other calves, as I noticed them licking the partition. Two of them also were grinding their teeth and one appeared starry-eyed. I moved closer. She was totally blind.

'Delwyn, when did you paint this place?'

'I can't remember. It must have been several years ago.'

My suspicions were partly answered.

'Your calves have lead poisoning. That paint is probably full of it. The older the paint, the more dangerous it seems to be.'

Delwyn was leaning against the wall on the other side.

'So that's what is killing my calves. I lost a couple from the fits last year.'

'We'll take some blood samples and send them away to be checked.'

Bill brought the BAL from our 'anti-disaster' medical bag. We treated all the calves in the pen. Delwyn was already making plans to remove and burn the wooden partition.

I was always happy to have students around. They kept me up to date with the academic work and I quietly enjoyed hearing about their escapades in the neighbourhood. Besides, they opened and closed the farm gates, prepared the medicine packets and bottles, and they often chauffeured me around the farms.

Bill had taken over the wheel as we tore out of the farm-yard on to the main road leaving behind a cloud of smoke.

'Look, there's Enoch, the Bobby. He is stopping us. O my God!'

Bill was as white as a sheet and trembled all over. Enoch was the village police sergeant and he recognized my car (or what was left of it).

'Hello, how about a ride to the village?'

'Of course. Jump in. You are out early this morning.'

As he climbed into the back seat, he told us about the farm lads up the valley. They had been caught by the water bailiff poaching salmon in the river Taf a few nights previously. He had caught them red-handed with a pot of 'jam' (the local term for an illegal concoction devised to lure the salmon). To make things worse, they had thrown him into the river. Enoch had been out to serve their summonses to appear in the local court the following week.

Bill drove us to the village without a word from his mouth and with his eyes glued to the road all the time. He even forgot his favourite Woodbine.

P.S. Enoch Jones thanked us and got on his way.

'Bill, are you feeling all right?' I enquired, since he still looked rather pale around the gills.

'All right, by golly, I was scared to death. You see, my driving licence has expired!'

I took over the driving and we continued our discussion of grass sickness.

'How did you manage to cure Sir Toli then?'

'Perseverance, my boy, and lots of good nursing. I expect Olwen told you how they attended to him around the clock for a couple of weeks.'

'She did. Her dad lived with him all the time.'

'Well, he is one of the family, isn't he?'

'Of course. What happens in this disease?'

'We don't really know. It affects horses when they are turned out to grass in the spring. The disease only occurs in the western regions of the island. Some cases develop acute colic and die within hours. Most develop a complete blockage of the large intestine and linger for several days or weeks. Very few recover.'

The morning sun had finally broken through as the mist cleared over the hill. We turned off the main road on to the farm lane lined with lilacs and rhododendrons. Bill's face was as red as a beetroot.

'Let's drop in to check up on Sir Toli. And maybe you would like to see what your girlfriend looks like in the morning!'

Continuing our discussion on the way home we turned to the art of ageing horses. Bill was well up on the subject, including my question about the expression 'Don't look a gift horse in the mouth.'

'It's because you tell the age of a horse by the teeth, so, it really means simply that you should not try to put a price on a gift—it is not cricket!'

'What about cows? Can you tell their age by the teeth?'

'Yes, but it is not so reliable. Very often eruption depends on the animal's state of nutrition. However, a simple way is to count the number of rings at the base of the horns and add two—if you can find one with horns nowadays!'

The Village of Gellywen.

Bill Hinds's farm had land on both sides of the River Tywi. The cows would swim
across in the morning and return when it was time for evening milking;
an excellent way to wash the udders!

Rest in Peace . . .

Esiah Jones lived with his spouse, Florrie, in a lonely farmhouse tucked neatly into the side of a bracken-covered hill overlooking a meandering stream. The farm was typical of many farmsteads in our practice area. Esiah had lived here all his life with his favourite herd of Shorthorn cattle—some red, some white, and some roan. A weather-worn, grey-haired son of the soil, Esiah was known to his neighbours as a quiet, God-fearing individual reputed to have put away a pretty useful 'nest egg' for a rainy day as the result of his own and his wife's endless toils. Indeed, down in the local village, they whispered that the old man was rather rich—'every penny a prisoner.'

In the old days, they built farmsteads where a good water supply was located. This meant that the farm lane would track across the length of several fields from the nearest public roadway—and invariably there were several gates to be opened and closed in transit! Such was the case with Esiah Jones's farm. A call to his farm on a cold, rainy night was not exactly a picnic, for invariably part of the lane was impassable and meant walking the rest of the way.

I well remember one such occasion when I was called to attend a cow which reportedly was trying to calve. The night was pitch black and the wind whistled in the hedgerows as I walked to the farm. All of a sudden, I heard a loud snort followed by the most deafening bellow I had ever heard—noises always seem louder in the night. I froze with horror, fright, and a sense of sheer helplessness—behind the hedgerow was Esiah Jones's ferocious bull. I have never been known for my athletic abilities, but Jim Thorpe in the prime of his glorious career never covered the 100 yard dash with the flashing speed that I took off for the farmhouse on that terrifying occasion.

I am usually a polite kind of person but this time, regard for personal safety took over. My flight for life ended by charging through the farmhouse kitchen door and almost ending in the lap of the farmer's wife who was seated in a rocking chair beside a crackling log fire.

When I had recovered my breath, I proceeded to explain my

predicament, only to be greeted with shrieks of laughter from the old farmer and his wife.

The purpose of my visit was a routine attention to a rather simple maternity case. Afterwards, I was escorted to my car, aboard the farmer's Fordson tractor.

Not many years had gone by when I was informed during a call in the neighbourhood that old Esiah Jones had passed away. It was my custom under such circumstances to visit and pay my respects to the family. A few days later I decided to pay such a visit to Florrie Jones whom I had admired along with her husband as fine, down-to-earth, hard-working, country folk.

I knocked at the kitchen door and the dear lady greeted me with her usual welcome. As always she wore a long frock down to her ankles, wooden clogs on her feet, a black shawl and a well-worn cap with the peak backwards. I was taken into the front parlour heavily furnished with antique furniture, Dresden china, and many ornaments that would be the envy of many a modern antique hunter.

'Will you have a cup of tea?'

'Yes, please, Mrs. Jones,' I had enjoyed many a fine meal at this farm after some tough cases.

'I also want you to read this,' said Florrie, handing me a long white envelope. I opened it, and took out a long document and proceeded to read it as my hostess went to the kitchen to prepare the tea.

I was rather flabbergasted to find that the document was a copy of her late husband's will.

Contrary to local gossip, the old man left her with very little money. The farm was heavily mortgaged and things looked pretty bad.

'What do you think of that?' snorted my hostess as she laid down a tray full of bread, butter, raspberry jam, gooseberry tart and a pot of tea, complete with its multi-coloured cosy.

I was rather speechless and muttered a few words.

'Well,' she said, 'if ever I can find enough money, I will place a tombstone over him with the inscription: 'Rest in Peace—until I come.'

Esiah Jones did just that for seventeen years when *she* finally was laid to rest. Can you imagine the furore that broke out at the Pearly Gates when Florrie Jones came charging in!

The Morgan Family: Bob, Menna, Richard, Ann, and Robert who succeeded his father in the Carmarthen practice. *Photo courtesy Ann Morgan.*

Joy and Sorrow in the Stable

The tempo of our practice was in high gear with the usual variety of end-of-winter ailments. It was early on a Saturday evening that I received a call to attend a mare which was having difficulty foaling. My partner was the horse specialist in our practice. I had been brought up on a dairy farm, and my interests were mainly with cattle. However, I also had a lot of love for horses. My dad had several farm horses, for tractors were not available in the 1930's in our area.

The horses always received special attention on our farm. There was Capten, a fine looking, bay gelding with the heart of a lion especially at hay harvest time. But he was also a mean rascal who was always handled by the head farm-worker. Duchess was a massive old girl, over sixteen hands tall. She did everything in her own sweet time. Then there was Bess, a darker bay and more of Welsh cob type. My favourite, however, was little Nancy, a chestnut-coloured Welsh cob mare. She was a faithful and reliable family pet. For many years she was assigned the daily task of delivering the milk to the creamery in the village about three miles away. She was carefully groomed and fed by John who worked for my Dad for over twenty years. John was a short, square-shouldered fellow who got along on one leg. He knew the names and the vital statistics of every boxing champion in history! Whenever he was sick or took a day off, my eldest brother would take over. The rest of us had to wait our turn, and I was only number four in the pecking order. It was quite a day when my Dad finally entrusted me with this plum assignment. My brothers had grown up to bigger and better things. It was a beautiful Easter Saturday. I had worked on Nancy the previous evening until her coat shone like a bottle, and the milk cart also had a special wash. I felt like a Roman emperor in his chariot as I sat on one of the milk churns while Nancy trotted briskly into the village. It was the first of many trips.

The thought of attending to my first foaling case was exasperating if not frightening. I had never even seen a foaling take place on our farm. Nearly every spring we had a new foal and sometimes two. It was always a custom to set up a vigil as soon as any of the mares showed signs of impending foaling. The most reliable sign is the appearance of drops of colostrum—first milk—on the tips of the mare's teats ('tops'). I had learned long ago the truth of the saying that a mare can produce a foal 'at the blink of an eyelid'. Somehow our mares always foaled during the short intervals they were not under our observation.

My student at this time was Henry. He was a city lad who loved horses. His great ambition was to become an equine specialist. He had never witnessed a foaling case either. Away we tore through the village. As we engaged the hill across the railway on the way out of the village I stopped to pick up my banker, Mr. Richard Harries, who was taking his customary evening stroll.

As usual, Saturday evening emergency calls always seem to be in the farthest corner of the practice. Even though this was only about seven miles, it took a while to engage the steep hills and the horseshoe bends. This one was no different, but the journey gave us an opportunity to chat with the banker. Besides, this had been a very important week in the financial world.

'Well, Mr. Harries, what did you think of the Budget and the extra shilling on a packet of cigarettes?' enquired my understudy with his usual interest in world affairs.

'I was rather intrigued by this new term that the Chancellor introduced and talked about at length.'

'Oh, you mean the term 'inflation'?'

'That's it. Tell us more about it.'

'I like the Chancellor's definition, but I am scared of its effects.'

'Such as—'

'He defined it rather well, I thought, namely, too much money chasing after too few goods. Prices will rise and the economy will suffer. I am afraid we are going to hear a lot about inflation for many years.'

'The day of honest work for honest pay appears to be disappearing,' Mr. Harries remarked as we drove into Jim Rees's farmyard.

Our client was anxiously waiting for us at the stable door. He doffed his cap nervously when I introduced our distinguished guest. Our patient was Bess, a massive dappled grey Shire mare.

'She's had tops on her teats for several days and became restless this afternoon. I thought it would be better to call you before dark.'

Jim had been a faithful client for many years, and I was especially grateful that my baptism in foaling cases should be with such a kind and considerate gentleman. I was nervous too.

The grey mare was obviously very uncomfortable as sweat poured out all over her. Jim's wife, Martha, had anticipated our needs as she appeared with a bucketful of warm water, soap and a towel. Henry checked her pulse and mucous membranes and held her tail to one side while Jim was assigned the arduous task of picking up and holding one fore leg. Though most farm mares are very docile, we took no chances, to prevent her kicking.

Part of the placenta was already showing as I proceeded to examine her per vagina.

'Be careful she doesn't break your arm,' gasped Mrs. Rees. 'That's what happened to our neighbour when he tried his hand at it last week.'

I assured her that I would exercise great care. I had been warned by my partner many times about the tremendous force produced by a straining mare. I proceeded to explain to Henry that I was being very careful not to get my arm caught between the foal and the mare's pelvis when she was straining. The cardinal rule is to carry out manipulation of the foal *in between* the straining movements.

Fortunately, this was a fairly easy maternity case. My examination revealed that the foal was coming in the normal anterior presentation with the front feet in the vagina. However, the head was in the nape position—the front of the nose was pressing against the entrance to the pelvis. This is a fairly common cause of dystocia, or difficult birth in a mare since a foal has a long narrow face. Unless it negotiates the vagina in a fairly horizontal direction, there is usually trouble.

While my patient relaxed in between her futile efforts to deliver her foal, I pushed the head away from the pelvic entrance and quickly lifted it into the vagina. I had already learned after several dystocias in cattle that successful delivery depended more on the right push or pull in the right direction at the right time than on brute strength.

Almost immediately Bess gave a massive heave and soon her foal saw the light of day almost like a shot from a gun. There he was with a beautiful white stripe all the way from his forehead to the tip of his nose and his umbilical cord still attached. Henry brought the tincture of iodine and some suitable nylon suture material to tie off the cord. We waited a while in order for the considerable volume of blood which was still in the umbilical cord to be returned to the foal. This is a very important procedure for otherwise this loss of blood could cause a relative anaemia in the foal and affect his brain. This is the basis of the 'sleeper foal syndrome'.

Martha brought the customary bucketful of hot bran mash for the new mother and the foal was soon wobbling to his feet. Our banker surveyed the scene with utter amazement and mused at the wonders of nature.

In the meantime, Jim had disappeared, but soon returned with his favourite Welsh Collie bitch in his arms.

'I am sorry it's late in the evening, but I wonder if you would mind checking Ffan for me. She has this horrible lump on her udder.'

It really was a sorry mess, and poor Ffan had obviously been ailing for a long time. The smell was almost unbearable.

'How old is she, Jim?'

Jim raised his cap and, scratching the side of his forehead, he recalled that she was as old as his youngest daughter—fifteen years and three months.

I explained to him that Ffan had a malignant tumour which had probably spread to her internal organs. We could remove the tumour, but it was obviously too late. Unfortunately, this was one of many similar cases that I encountered in farm dogs throughout the years.

Henry prepared the euthanasia solution, and soon Ffan was in the land of eternal dreams.

We drove out of the farm yard and climbed the steep bumpy lane to the roadway. It was a gorgeous evening as the setting sun shone through the bushes which lined most of the farm lanes. It had been raining most of the day, but, as so often happened, the sun managed to come through about tea time. On such occasions the birds seem to sing better and the flowers certainly look fresher and enrich the evening air with a delightful aroma. This particular evening was no exception.

Who cared about the Budget when you had all of these gifts of nature? Even our banking guest forgot the burdens of his office.

Our conversation soon focused on our many blessings. He and I had both been brought up in the country during the Depression which really was not so bad after all. There was always plenty of home-produced food and every farmer claimed he had the best supply of bacon in the parish. In those days the fatter the bacon the better it was, and no one worried a hoot about cholesterol. Besides, there was no reason for alarm. Most farmers worked hard and lived to a ripe old age.

It was on this happy note that we dropped in on Ifor Morgans. I had spent many hours with his sick foal that developed swollen joints about ten days after he was born. Infection had got in through the navel cord at birth. I became a firm believer in the iodine treatment for the cord after this unhappy experience. Ifor was leaning over the stable door with his wife, Gwendoline, beside him, holding her apron to her face. Cold sweat broke out all over me. I knew the battle was over, lost after many days and nights of vigil by this devoted couple. As I gazed over the stable door, I saw him, lying in the straw. His eyes were wide open, but not a breath was left in him.

My client was a superb horseman. He had been around horses all his life and was well-known throughout the land for his fine show stock. This little filly was from his best Welsh Cob. I shared his grief as he wept unashamedly. We all shed a tear even if we didn't show it.

Such was life among these beautiful hills and vales. From pure ecstasy at the successful birth one hour to the depth of despair the next. It was a tough schooling for young Henry.

Mr. Harries, the Banker had much to contemplate over the next few weeks. He became acutely aware, at first hand, of some of the trials and tribulations of the farmer.

As for Ifor and his wife, they were the salt of the earth. Their faith saw them through to better days.

The Plants Wilted

There was nothing unusual about the Tuesday morning I drove into Bryn Farm to attend to a lame cow. Evan Williams was a middle-aged man with a perpetual red face which gave him the nickname of 'Full Moon'. He farmed as a sideline and his real interest was in politics. He had succeeded to win the local seat in the recent County Council election in the face of tough opposition. His victory was all the more surprising since he was a government inspector during the war and had the unenviable assignment to see that the local farmers planted their quota of crops. The destiny of the United Kingdom depended enormously on the increased production of food to offset the ravaging of our merchant ships by German U-boats.

While I was giving my patient an intraveneous injection of a new sulpha drug for 'foul in the foot'—an infection between the claws, Josh Davies, a neighbouring farmer, arrived. I inquired, 'Well, Josh, what's the topline news this morning?' He was the encyclopaedia of local gossip! Puffing hard on his pipe he replied, 'Well, Jack and Flo Harries have gone to London.'

'Jack and Flo gone to London!' interjected Evan as he removed his old trilby hat and wiped his bald head. 'That's a tall story if ever I heard one!' I agreed, because I knew the couple very well. They did not have a telephone but there was one in the kiosk nearby. Whenever our phone rang before 8:00 a.m. and I heard a coin dropping, I was pretty sure it was Jack calling about a sick cow. They were home birds who probably had never been further than Carmarthen.

As I was putting away my equipment in the boot of my car, Evan's wife, Sally, drove in. She had been to Cheerio Shop in the village which was a grocery store and Post Office. She remarked, 'There's a rumour in the village that Jack and Flo Harries have gone to London without telling a soul about their trip; also that their nephew had taken them to the station and then had taken their 10 cows to his farm until they came home.'

Over the next few days the rumours kept mounting and there was much apprehension. The local vet is usually well-informed on local news. Eventually I became very concerned about my esteemed clients and conveyed my feelings to the policeman who had now been posted on duty at the farm—also to the local news reporter. The news had now spread far and wide and Scotland Yard was called in. The Detective Inspector assigned to the case soon got down to business. After studying the situation he called for an extensive search of the area for several miles on the following Sunday. Hundreds of volunteers turned out from the farms and the villages. Dusk arrived and the search was discontinued.

However, it was now obvious that the Inspector and his associates had a hunch about the whereabouts of the couple. Early the following morning, they visited the nephew's farm. Someone had noticed that the kale plants (winter fodder) in one corner of the field had wilted. They decided to explore this area and soon uncovered the bodies of Jack and Flo. Both had been killed by a severe blow to the head.

The nephew was soon arrested and taken into custody. There was widespread rage that such a dreadful crime had been committed in our county where not even the policeman carried a gun. The wheels of justice moved fast. He was found guilty of murder and executed by hanging in Swansea Prison within a few months.

Daylight Saving Time

Daylight Saving Time has been the subject of considerable controversy in many lands ever since it was first adopted. There are often howls of protest when it's that time of year again. It seems there is confusion about which way the clock should be turned.

I well remember when I was a youngster attending chapel on a Sunday morning, with the deacons as usual siting in the big pew which is right at the front, directly below the pulpit. I have never been able to figure out whether they are there to keep an eye on the preacher or whether the preacher can see to it that they stay awake! Most of our deacons were elderly gentlemen with an air of sanctimony, dressed in black suits, fly collars, and flannel shirts. That particular Sunday morning the congregation was singing the last hymn with the usual Welsh fervour when old John Davies the blacksmith hobbled up the aisle on his walking stick and proceeded to make himself comfortable in his usual corner seat in the big pew.

The minister gave the closing benediction, the organist let forth with gusto on a piece from Handel while the congregation left for the usual Sunday dinner.

Poor old John Davies had forgotten to turn on his clock!

Talking about Daylight Saving Time, we really had it poured on us in Britain during World War II. We had to turn the clock on *two* hours in summer. It was almost too dark to get up in the morning and mothers chased their children to bed at what seemed to them to be an unearthly hour because of the daylight.

One beautiful evening in June, I was on the usual round of calls when a farmer's wife came out to the barn door breathless.

'Mr. Williams, your wife called. Please hurry to Evan Griffiths's farm—all his cows are sick!' Here again was one of the problems a vet has to ponder. What really is an emergency case? So often I used to rush to such calls and find the patient had been sick for several days. The fact is that there are *very few* real emergencies.

Evan Griffiths was a kind of a hermit who lived on his own in an old farmhouse on the other side of the valley. He milked a few cows, kept a few chickens, and wrote a lot of poetry.

I finished treating Jim Harries's lame bull and dashed to the 'emergency' in Evan's place. When I arrived on the yard, Evan was still trying to chase a few of the cows into the yard.

'Mr. Williams *bach*, I am so glad to see you. I have had a terrible time getting these cows in. They were all right when I turned them out last night.'

Evan and I and his Collie dog finally rounded up all the cows. I checked a few but none seemed to be sick and it was obvious they had no milk. I could see that Evan was stomping back and forth and looking up at the sky. 'What's the matter, Evan? Are you checking up on the weather?' 'No, not really—but, what time is it?

Evan's mouth dropped wide open as he pulled out his watch and in a loud voice exclaimed, 'Mercy, mercy, it's only ten o'clock!'

Old Evan had finished the evening milking and had an early supper as usual. As was his custom, he went to bed early because he was also an early riser. That evening he had fallen asleep and woke up to find it was daylight.

So, he rushed out of bed and fetched in the cows!

The cows went back to pasture, the moon came up over the forest—and Evan Griffiths went back to bed.

They Come By Moonlight

That Friday evening late in July, I went to bed rather tired and looked forward to a slightly more relaxed weekend. It had been an unusually heavy week and that afternoon I had taken time to attend the funeral of a dear friend. As so often happened under such conditions, within 10 minutes I was on my way to attend a cow with maternity problems. It is also a strange fact that night calls are never just down the road—this one was at the furthest end of the practice about 17 miles away. That was quite a distance in those days. Another significant fact is that invariably such a call would be to a farm off the main road.

I drove up hill and down dale and the final couple of miles along the coastline. The farm was located near the sea and as I walked the final half mile, I could hear the waves breaking against the rocks as the moon climbed slowly over the cliffs in the distance. I was greeted by the anxious owner and the usual gallery of neighbours. We entered the barn which was really a small shed made of corrugated iron and a dirt floor. My patient was standing in the corner and I could see that she was trying to produce a calf.

'How long has she been like this?' I enquired.

My client was a quiet-spoken, hard-working person with a houseful of young children. His farm was not exactly the best but he was managing to make ends meet through sheer guts and toil. All the people in this coastline region had their unique accent known to the rest of us as the 'dewn-belew' kind since their pronunciation of words was so different—they really mean 'down below.'

'Well, I reck-on she 'as been leik this for queit a wheil—since this morning.'

I also find it hard to understand that in this kind of situation, there is always a tendency to wait until near midnight or later before calling for help. Incidentally, folks in this area also figure that cattle (and women) produce their young when the tide comes in!

The farmer's wife brought the requested bucket of warm water, soap and towel while I stripped to my waist and donned my rubber overall which was ideally suitable apparel for delivering calves. My patient was a small Friesian heifer and it seemed by the size of the feet that her calf was as big as she was! This situation often happens. Cattle reach puberty at 6 to 8 months of age but should never be bred until they are at least 15 months. While the owner may have good intentions, invariably it's the neighbour's bull that is usually the culprit—and the worse looking mongrel type (as in all species) is usually the most fertile!

I examined the heifer and it was obvious the calf was already dead. We applied chains to the front legs and beckoned our helpers to get on the end and pull. It was to no avail.

'It's no use, Mr. Harries, we will have to cut the calf out piece by piece.' Nowadays, a Caesarean operation would be performed but the law in those days required a general anaesthetic for a major operation. Cows were not good patients under those circumstances.

I walked back to the car and collected my instruments. I knew we were set for a long, hard night.

The operation is known as embryotomy or fetotomy and is an endurance test for man and beast.

The procedure is always easier with the cow standing and an injection into the epidural space in the spine near the root of the tail stops the animal from straining and makes the operation easier for all concerned.

I passed a loop of wire so as to encompass the head and neck and one front limb behind the shoulder and brought the two ends out through the embryotomy tube to prevent damage to the vagina. One of the lusty farmers at hand was then instructed to saw the wire so as to split the calf's fore quarters. This is tough work, for the calf's bones are pretty thick and hard even at this age.

Section by section the procedure was repeated—across the calf's trunk and the other foreleg, until only the hind quarters were left.

By this time the poor heifer was tired and down she went in the straw! That made the operation doubly difficult!

'How about a cup of tea?' chirped a quiet voice as the barn door opened. A little lady entered with a tray of sandwiches and tea. Believe me, any refreshments under these circumstances are a real banquet. We all sat in the straw and thoroughly enjoyed the hospitality. I have a feeling that the poor heifer enjoyed the rest also!

The feast was soon over and we returned to our task. After some more, tedious hours, we finally succeeded in delivering all the pieces.

'It's four o'clock in the morning!' said one of the neighbours, dusting off his pocket watch.

'Too early for milking,' said another.

'That's right,' said my client. 'We haven't finished yet. Would you mind having a look at this calf?' as he led me to another shed, followed by our band of neighbours.

'He has had that lump on his jaw for several days and I was going to call you sometime.'

The light in the barn was not the best but I managed to look into his mouth and saw two large ulcers on the gum, coated with cheese-like material.

'Ah, Mr. Harries, this is a case of calf diphtheria.'

'What did ye s-a-y? D-ip-th-eria!'

'Oh no, not like the human type! It's a name for an infection in the mouth caused by the same germ as in foot rot. A little sulphonamide powder medication will fix that.'

I was tired out and longed to be on the way back to my warm bed.

'Breakfast is ready!' came a voice from the kitchen door. This was it! No sleep last night or this morning!

We all trooped into the house and sat down on the hard wooden stools around the kitchen table which had been carefully laid with the best china. There were bacon, eggs, bread and butter, marmalade, and plenty of tea.

Now no matter how hard the job or how late the hour, there is nothing to compare with a farmhouse breakfast and a chat with a group of clients. Time is meaningless as the topics of conversation range from a discussion of the latest neighbourhood scandal to national politics. I have often enjoyed listening to (and sometimes participating in) many fine and occasionally heated arguments on many varied topics.

All too soon, it *was* time for milking. I gathered my equipment, left the farmyard and crossed the fields to my car, accompanied by Mr.

Harries. The sun was already burning brightly in the horizon. It was a wonderful sight. The birds were singing their praises to another daybreak and a light mist covered the bare cliffs.

'Let me know about her in a day or two,' I told my client as I warmed up my Ford car and reversed on to the highway. I drove along the coastline and stopped at a suitable vantage point to breathe the morning air. Down below, the sea was calm and the waves broke lightly over the pebbly beach, while the seagulls hopped and fluttered from rock to rock and others took their morning bath in the ocean. Everything was so peaceful and beautiful—but soon the crowds would come and change the whole spectacle.

I drove back to the surgery and checked the daybook for the morning calls—a sick dog coming in at 11 o'clock, two calls on the north side of the practice and several odds and ends. This was obviously going to be another busy day.

I was young and rather energetic in those days. Even though the day was a busy one it was Saturday and my evening for recreation—if I could find the time. What is more, these were still the days of petrol rationing in the immediate post war era. The penalties for misuse were rather harsh. Even though my fiancée was a farmer's daughter, it was hard to find an excuse that there was a sick animal at the farm every Saturday night. The village Bobby knew better, though I must admit it was the usual alibi on a wet or snowy occasion!

There was nothing for it but to use a bicycle. My bicycle was borrowed from Menna, the boss's wife and the trip to the farm was a delightful six mile ride through the valley—at least it was rather pleasant on the way up but rather tedious coming home early on Sunday morning!

I finally crawled into bed as another day was dawning—about thirty hours since that call on the Friday evening. Such was the wonderful, colourful life of a young country vet.

Prince Philip, the Duke of Edinburgh presenting the Silcock Gold Cup for the best dairy herd in England and Wales in 1956, to Dyfrig and Iorwerth.

Grove Farm today.

Arsenic in the Rice Pudding

The scene on the farmyard at Nant-y-gwr on that black Monday morning was enough to turn the stomach of the toughest vet. I have been blessed with an unruffled disposition, but this one really was as much as I could take. I have a deep passion for animals and great respect for my clients.

I had arrived at the farm along with my student, David, at the crack of dawn on a gorgeous sunny day in July. (The summer had been most agreeable—no rain for a week!)

Daniel Davies had gone out to fetch his milk cows as usual. You can imagine his bewilderment on finding several dead, others obviously sick and some missing somewhere in the woods.

Our flight to the farm—it seems that our little Ford car seemed to be airborne most of the way—was accomplished in record time, but already a couple more had collapsed and died on the farmyard. This was one of the best dairy herds in the country and the owner was a highly respected farmer.

'Heavens above! What a mess!' David remarked.

Daniel had gone into the woods to search for the missing ones while his wife, two daughters, and the hired help were trying to get some order into the milking line. After all, the milk lorry was due to arrive in an hour to collect the milk for the creamery—but none would be available from that morning's supply.

David and I put on our overboots and proceeded to examine the stock. The dead ones gave us little help on superficial examination. There were several down on the yard and some managed to stumble to their feet after much effort. Others were on their feet but staggered as they moved across the yard. They kicked at their abdomen and grinded their teeth—a sure sign of 'gutsache' in cattle, and several had very obvious diarrhoea.

David went back to our car which housed our mobile clinic, complete with syringes, medicine, etc., and a set of post-mortem knives. 'The key to the living is often found in the dead' could well be a pathologist's motto. David brought the knives and we proceeded to open up one carcass to search for some clues.

The internal organs were all pretty congested and the lining of the gut was extremely inflamed.

By this time our client had returned. 'Daniel, what's been going on here lately?'

'Nothing unusual, as far as I know.'

'Have you checked the calves and heifers?'

'Yes, they appear to be all right.'

'Then it must be something confined to the milking herd. Let's see, have you changed their feed lately?'

'No, not at all.'

'Some of these cows are trying to lick their backs which seems to hurt them.'

We examined the skin over this area and it was obviously very inflamed. By this time, Daniel had recovered from the initial shock of seeing the state of his prize stock and he remarked,

'You know, the flies were bothering the cows more than usual when they came in last night. I remembered that I had some stuff up in the loft which I had bought at a farm sale several years ago. It was a kind of fly spray so I brought it down and rubbed it into the cows' backs after milking.'

Daniel Davies produced an empty can but the label had been destroyed.

'It smells like phenol,' said my alert student.

'Right, and that would certainly burn their skin. Are you sure this is really a fly spray?' I hated to bother poor Daniel too much but we had to get to the root of the problem.

'I am not sure.'

David, in the meantime, had checked the farm cats and dogs that he could find, and reported that they appeared to be normal.

'This is obviously a case of poisoning of some sort. David, let's collect some specimens of liver, kidney, and bowel content, and rush them to the County Laboratory for examination—and let's not forget to get some morning milk samples as well.'

We called my colleagues in the practice to send some help, for the sick animals had to be treated symptomatically until we could solve the case and apply any specific treatment that might be available. We had a pretty good idea of the cause but wanted a definite diagnosis if possible. David stayed on the farm to start the fluid therapy. I racked my brain for all the likely poisons as I sped to the laboratory.

I was able to get quick attention at the lab and the result was soon known—phenol and arsenic!

'Whew! That was not fly spray—those are the ingredients of a sheep dip!'

It was the custom to dip sheep once a year against skin and wool parasites.

I picked up the phone and called the farm. Sarah Davies answered.

'Hello, I have the report for you.'

'Yes, yes—what is it?' she enquired nervously.

'Mrs. Davies, that stuff you rubbed on the cows' backs contained arsenic!'

The Grove Boys: Eric, Huw, Iorwerth, Awstin and Dyfrig (mid 1950s).

Her answer in Welsh was unprintable—and then there was a slight pause.

'Oh, thank you so much. I know I should not have done it, but I used some of the milk to make rice pudding!'

'Well, Mrs. Davies, thank Heavens it's not time for lunch. You better get rid of it—and don't forget, don't give it to the cats or dogs either!'

We worked on Daniel Davies' herd for many days. It was a tragic event. But, the courage and fortitude with which this fine family faced their horrible ordeal was an example I will never forget. Out of adversity, I gained the most respected client relationship I have ever known.

Daniel Davies weathered the storm of having lost so many of his stock. He continued to farm with his usual skill and diligence. There is something about country folk that is rarely found in other walks of life—faith in their eventual destiny.

The story of the 'arsenic in the rice pudding' travelled across the land, far and wide. It certainly had its moral.

The Chapel in the Valley

Autumn, 'the season of mists and mellow fruits', was here again. It had been an interesting day which Andrew and I had spent tuberculin testing three herds of cattle, attending a horse with colic, delivering twin calves, vaccinating some puppies against distemper and a few other routine calls. This was scheduled to be one of our infrequent nights off duty, and we were cruising down the horse-shoe bend into the valley. Dusk was falling as the sun was setting like a ball of fire behind the Frenni mountain.

We pulled up and stood on the hedge overlooking the village. The whole valley was a gorgeous carousel of autumn colours. It had been a beautiful sunny day and now there was not even a breeze. Once again, some of those lines from Grey's *Elegy in a Country Churchyard* which I had forced myself to memorize in school assumed a new and wonderful meaning:

> *'The curfew tolls the knell of parting day,*
> *The lowing herds wind slowly o'er the lea*
> *The ploughman homeward plods his weary way*
> *And leaves the world to darkness and to me.'*

Meanwhile, cars had been converging on the village from both directions. Ceinwen Evans had informed us, while she served her favourite blackberry tart and cream after we had delivered twin calves, that tonight they were holding their annual harvest thanksgiving service at her chapel.

'I have heard a lot about Welsh singing. Do you think we could stop in for a while?' enquired Andrew as he viewed the activity below. Andrew was a city lad from the heart of England.

Being an avid music lover, I wasted no time in getting the old Ford down the hill, and soon we were entering the little chapel. It was almost full, but Hannah Morris beckoned us to join her and her family in the back corner pew.

One side of the gallery was occupied by the farm lads who winked at the girls on the other side. Sally Hughes, the local dressmaker, presided at the organ near the pulpit. She was a short, stubby little soul who played the customary Handel's *Largo* with a sanctimonious air. Soon, the door alongside the pulpit opened and in came the Minister followed by the guest preacher, the Ministers from the neighbouring chapels, the Vicar and the deacons. Harvest thanksgiving services are traditionally truly ecumenical occasions. They all perched themselves in the big pew under the pulpit.

The opening hymn was introduced by the Congregational minister who read the verses with great deliberation. The singing was conducted by Dilwyn Meredith, the local carpenter. He really looked the part in his Sunday best tweed suit, flannel shirt with a 'come to Jesus collar' and a Hallelujah tie. Dilwyn was still a bachelor, but by all accounts he had quite a crush on the organist, but so far, to no avail.

The singing was absolutely superb as the whole congregation poured forth in melodious voice. Up in the corner of the gallery among the tenors was Cyril Bowen, the butcher—a short, round little fellow in his Sunday best tweeds and a flaming red waistcoat. He was singing so hard the veins on his temple seemed as if they would burst any minute, while over in the other corner, among the bass, there was tall, lanky Jacob Owen, the grocer. His Adam's Apple bobbed up and down like a yo-yo. My favourite was Martha Jones, better known as 'Martha rhubarb' because she always won first prize at the Show for her rhubarb. She opened her mouth so wide you could almost see her tonsils.

The Presbyterian minister read the lesson and he was followed by the Vicar who gave the prayer. Seated in front of us was Lisa Phillips who had her hands full trying to control her five children. She reminded me of my dear mother who was often in the same predicament. During a pause in the prayer, one of her kids leaned over the back of the seat and whispered rather loudly, 'Mr. Williams, the old sow had ten pigs.'

The highlight of the evening was the sermon. The guest preacher was a very handsome young man who had recently accepted the 'call' to this chapel. His appearance in the pulpit was in itself an inspiration. He started by reading his text, chosen from the Psalms. It was then repeated in English. Otherwise, the sermon was totally in Welsh. It was a real masterpiece which lasted for sixty five minutes (duly timed by my student!). This was the era of outstanding performance from the pulpits across the land. This young minister gave a brilliant analysis of some of the social problems of the day magnificently illustrated by many well selected quotations from the Scripture. Time was immaterial since all the congregation was obviously held spellbound. Even old Simon concentrated more on the sermon than on his organist! As the preacher worked his sermon towards the climax, his voice grew more melodious and eventually reached the unique technique adopted by most of the star performers of the Cloth in those days, whereby the sermon becomes almost a treatise in song.

Andrew was obviously fascinated—if not bewildered—by this superb artistry, but I believe he derived much amusement from the Ministers and deacons who indulged in another custom of yesteryear whereby they greeted every profound exposition of the gospel with a low chorus of Amens, which became more frequent as the preacher drove home his message.

Judging by the collection plates, it was obvious that the preacher had stirred the congregation to give until it made them feel good!

The closing hymn was one of my favourites and a fitting climax to a truly inspiring evening. The English equivalent is:

'*We plough the fields and scatter the good seed on the land . . .*'

As usual, the whole congregation sang their hearts out, and to Andrew's delight, repeated the last couple of lines of the last verse three times—again according to the 'big occasion' custom.

We descended the steps into the village, amid many handshakes from clients and non-clients who were rather surprised by our presence. John Hughes gave us an up-to-date report on his sick grey mare; Fannie Jones's Jersey cow needed another visit the next day, while little Bethan Owen was delighted that we had saved her pet lamb. Oliver Hughes insisted on telling us his latest juicy story which he had picked up at the cattle market, and Andrew lined up a date with a lovely brunette from Nant Farm. But alas, the epilogue was yet to be played!

In a rural community, the local vet's car and its licence number is known to most people. For some reason, my colleagues and I had the questionable reputation of being reckless speedsters, though I was convinced our particular vehicle had more noise than speed. Hence, our trek up and down the countryside never went unnoticed.

On this particular evening, Elwyn Rees had decided it was time to phone for the vet. His prize Welsh Corgi bitch had delivered one live puppy in the afternoon, but nothing else happened. On his way to the telephone kiosk, he spotted our car and finally, when the crowd began to disperse, he converged on us with an eloquent plea for help.

So ended our evening off—performing a Caesarean in Elwyn's garage. Poor Andrew, he had to come also! Professional duty always comes first. He could sow his wild oats another day!

F&M: TB

We were cleaning up the instruments in the corner of the barn after a tough calving case on Evan Hughes' farm when an excited neighbour crashed through the door. He almost landed on his face in the cow manure.

'What's all the excitement?' enquired my bewildered client.

'Mr. Vet — Vet, have you heard the news?'

'What news? Settle down. Who's dead?'

'No-one, but it is te-rri-ble!'

'Well, let's have it.'

'My wife came back from the village. She heard at the butcher's shop that foot-and-mouth disease has been found in the county!'

'Whew! Is that right? John, run to the house and call the police station to find out.'

John, the twinkle-toed son of my client, took off like a rocket. In no time I heard him shout, 'Yes, the police said it's at Jim Owen's farm near Carmarthen.'

'Hm, that's only six miles away!'

There was a tense silence. We gathered our instruments and walked pensively to our car. It was as if the plague had struck right there. We all knew the implications of this horrible disease.

I bid Evan Hughes and his son good day and left them gazing helplessly on the cobbled yard. I could read his mind—would it strike at his cows?

We were out on the highway heading for home when David, my second-year student, finally broke the uneasy silence.

'Have you had foot-and-mouth here before?'

'Not for many years, fortunately. Believe me, it's a terrible disease. Have you had lectures on it yet?'

'No, except a little about the virus.'

We drove along and I started to indoctrinate my young colleague on the ravages of foot-and-mouth disease.

I explained that the disease does not kill many cattle but it spreads like lightning. It affects all cloven-hoofed animals—cattle, sheep, pigs, etc.—but not horses, dogs or cats. It can be spread very easily by human clothes, boots, car tyres, etc. Even the wind and birds can convey the virus from one farm to the other.

'What will happen now?'

'Well, all cloven-footed animals on the farm will have to be destroyed and the buildings thoroughly disinfected. The farmer and his family will have to stay at home and no one will be allowed to enter the premises. A policeman will be on duty at the farm entrance all the time.'

'What about food—and the mail?'

'They will have to be left at the farm entrance.'

'How will they dispose of the dead ones—can you eat them?'

'Now, now, you are not that stupid! Heavens no! no! That would be a sure way of spreading the disease. The carcasses have to be burned or buried deep in lime. Probably this outbreak came from imported meat.'

'How would that get to Mr. Owen's farm?'

'I don't know the details yet; he raises a lot of pigs and collects kitchen refuse from the nearest village to feed them.'

'You mean left-over meat, etc., get thrown in with the kitchen waste? Isn't there a law which says that all swill has to be cooked before feeding it?'

'Glad to hear you say that. You are right, but—'

We reached home and found a group of farmers discussing the big news with Olwen Jones, our office manager. Before long my surgery was overcrowded with farmers and half the street neighbours wanting to know the latest.

Enoch Davies the baker wondered if his shop would be closed, while James Mitchell the banker worried about the economy.

'You fellows will have to stay home for a while now. There will be no movement of animals within a nine mile radius of the affected farm until the disease has been cleared out.'

I could see the sudden change that came across the faces of my clients. Emlyn Court always looked forward to Wednesdays—it was the big cattle market day in Carmarthen and he made the rounds of the local pubs all the way home. He was so drunk one night he lost his false teeth!

'Will I be able to go courting?' asked Ianto Hughes, who farmed with his dad and was a wild young lover.

'Depends where you want to go.'

He blushed from ear to foot. He was dating Mr. Owen's eldest daughter.

'Not for at least a few weeks, Ianto.'

'This village will be as dead as a doornail,' sighed Jack Williams the butcher.

He had visions of closing down his business, but I reassured him that the team of government vets was highly trained to deal with an outbreak and that it would soon be under control.

'All concerts and whist drives should be cancelled,' demanded Rev. Paul Jones the Vicar.

'And the morning service!' chuckled Davy Hughes.

'Why?' came a chorus from the back.

'That's a good point, Vicar,' I remarked. 'The less people move around, the sooner we will get this mess under control.'

'Why don't they vaccinate the animals? Do we *have* to slaughter them?'

'I'm afraid so. We do have a vaccine but it does not cover all types of viruses that can cause foot-and-mouth. Also, all the animals, I mean cattle, would have to be vaccinated twice a year and that would be very expensive. Besides, this country has been free from foot-and-mouth for many years. You don't get rid of any disease by vaccinating. You just control it.'

'Why do most cases occur in the autumn?'

'That's a good question, Mr. Pugh. I believe it's because the disease is brought over from France by birds—starlings. I was over there, as you know, last year and I actually visited a farm with foot-and-mouth with the local vet who wanted me to see it.'

There was this cow standing there, slobbering, chomping her jaws, and she was very lame. I looked around and there were several like her. In fact, I have a film of the cows. I did not go on the field.'

'Don't they have laws like ours?'

'Unfortunately, no. At least, not in that part of France. So no wonder we have problems with the birds. However, I must say that they are now doing something about it.'

'Will Mr. Owen get paid for his stock?' enquired Thomas Griffiths the grocer.

'Oh yes. Very reasonably, usually. He can re-stock in about six weeks. In the meantime, he might as well go to the South of France for a holiday.'

It turned out that David Owen had bought a cow at the local market which had been brought from Cheshire. She had come down with the disease a few days later. This created a terrible problem. Every animal that was in the market that day had to be traced. Besides, how many farmers or dealers or just onlookers might have carried the disease home with them on their boots or clothes? It was an anxious time for all of us. Our practice was almost at a standstill. That's when I really began to appreciate the fact that I had been trained to be a vet for *all* animals, even though horses and cows were my most frequent patients.

My student was recruited to join the foot-and-mouth team and was excused from returning to college until the disease was controlled. Swarms of ministry-employed vets were drafted into the neighbourhood from all parts of the country to trace the stock sold from the local market. Others visited Mr. Owen's neighbouring farms for several days to check their animals in case they would come down with the disease.

Fortunately, there were no further outbreaks and loud was the praise for my noble profession for a magnificent operation. My heart was full of pride, even though I was not directly involved. The foot-and-mouth disease programme had come under harsh criticism from several media, but I am thoroughly convinced it has stood the test of time.

Soon our practice was in full swing again—in fact, it was almost a twenty-four hour a day operation to clear up some of the long waiting list of routine cases.

As for Ianto Hughes—well, the poor fellow lost out! His girl married a vet from the government!

*   *   *

Malcolm, my student, and I were returning home after a very busy day tuberculin testing several dairy herds. It was a typical wet Monday but it was also winter time when the milk cows were housed all the time, from November until March. This made our work so much easier, especially for night calls for dystocia because the cowsheds were nice and warm.

'Well, young man, have you done your homework on tuberculosis?' —his assignment for the past week.

'Yes, I am ready.' Tuberculosis, also known as 'consumption' in humans is caused by a germ, *Mycobacterium tuberculosis*. It was discovered by Robert Koch, a German bacteriologist in the nineteenth century.

'How prevalent is the disease?'

'It occurs world wide and can affect all domestic animals and humans.'

'How do they become infected?'

'By inhalation or ingestion. In cattle, following inhalation the germs settle in the lymph nodes in the throat area and/or in the lungs where the classical picture is the formation of lesions known as tubercles or nodules which slowly enlarge. Several may coalesce (join together) and eventually rupture. Subsequent coughing will result in the spread of the infection in the sputum. Often this stage is not reached for several months or years. It has been referred to as a disease of advancing years and superdomestication.'

'How else can humans and animals become infected?'

'Calves by drinking infected milk. The same is true for us if we drink raw milk that may be carrying the germs. Pasteurizing the milk will kill the germs.'

'Koch studied filtrates from the culture of tubercle germs and he was convinced that he had found the means to cure the disease. This was not the case, but his work on TB filtrate paved the way for the production of tuberculin which we have been using today. By the widespread use of the tuberclin test, the disease will hopefully be eradicated.'

Update: Alexander Fleming discovered the antibiotic, penicillin, in 1929. In 1941 Howard Florey and Ernst Chain made studies which convinced them that penicillin had great therapeutic potential but realized that it could not be made in large quantities in the laboratory. Florey and Chain transferred their work to the U.S. This also led to the discovery of streptomycin in 1944 from streptomycin griseus. Other strains of streptomyces yielded additional therapeutic substances such as chloromycetin and aureomycin.

Today, tuberculosis can be treated effectively, especially in the early stages, by a combination of streptomycin, isoniazid and para-aminosalicylic acid. Even though TB had been almost eradicated in most countries, there has been a resurgence of the disease in humans and animals recently. In cattle it has been established that they can also acquire the disease from infected badgers.

Some Local Customs

As I reflect over the years, there are several customs that come to mind that are now extinct. My first recollection is of Hannah Morris, the itinerant seamstress who came for several days to prepare clothes for Mam and my sisters, usually in time for Easter. My brothers and I were assigned in turn to operate the sewing machine wheel for her and woe to us if we did not pay attention!

A big occasion on the farm was the annual pig slaughtering day. The parish butcher would come along and with the assistance of our farm servants he would soon have the job done. Boiling water was poured over the carcass and the hair removed by special hand scrapers. The internal organs were removed and the carcass hung in a cool building overnight. The ladies set about preparing faggots using minced liver, some pork and bread crumbs which were made into balls wrapped in pieces of 'the apron' which cover the intestines. The next day, the butcher returned to cut the carcass into several sections such as the shoulders, hams and sides which were then placed to soak in brine (salt and water) and some saltpetre solution. In about a week they were hung on hooks from the kitchen ceiling.

On New Year's Day, my brothers and I would visit our neighbours to wish them well in song for which we received *calennig* in the form of money, chocolates, or sweets. The farm servants would go singing around the neighbourhood during the night soon after the arrival of the New Year. Sometimes some farm girls would anticipate their arrival and pour a bucket of water over them from the bedroom window.

Funerals in the countryside were characterized by certain customs which were still in vogue during my childhood. The local carpenter brought the coffin which, after receiving the deceased, was placed on chairs in an upper room, sometimes surrounded by candles. The curtains were drawn in every room until after the funeral.

All work ceased on the farm except milking and feeding the livestock. Family members went to the tailor or dressmaker for black mourning clothes. For the servants and maids a black patch or band was sown on a sleeve.

The funeral service was conducted by the Minister or Vicar, assisted by his colleagues from the neighbourhood. In turn they expounded, often at length, on the virtues of the deceased to an overflowing congregation. The hymn singing was truly inspirational especially the traditional one at the graveside. Throughout the service and for the following two or three Sunday services, the family mourners remained seated.

A custom which dates from the seventeenth century was known as *Noson Lawen* (A Night of Happiness). Farms were small and isolated and the long days of summer gave little opportunity for community life. With the shorter winter days came more leisure time and long evenings. However, the good neighbourliness of that era led to gatherings in the big kitchen of one of the larger farms for poetry reciting, song and dance to the music of a Welsh harp. Eventually they were replaced by village concerts, *eisteddfodau* and nowadays radio, the cinema and television.

Client Psychology

I was busy writing up the previous day's visits when the phone rang.

'Is the vet there?' came a sulken voice from the other end.

'Yes, can I help you?'

'Are you the young pup who killed Esther Owen's horse?'

'What do you mean?'

'Well, she died, didn't she?'

'Yes, I suppose she did but—'

'I am not interested in you. I want a real vet—Mr. Morgan. He always takes care of my animals.'

'Sorry, he is not here today—but I will be glad to come out.'

'Hm, might as well shoot her now!'

'At least I can take a look,' I sighed, holding back my deep anger.

'Oh, all right. But you better not mess around with *my* animals.'

'We're on our way, Mr. Harries.'

My student, Jim, was standing nearby mixing up the usual quota of medicines for the daily rounds.

'Who on earth was that?'

'Some character who had swallowed another neighbourhood tale.'

'Did he say you killed Esther Owen's horse?'

'Yes.'

'Hm, I would have told him to go to hell. I wouldn't stand for that. Besides, that horse was dead before you even touched her and you told them so.'

'It makes no difference, Jim. Even though she had been sick for over a week and everyone else in the neighbourhood had tried his magic medicine, it's the poor vet who always gets the blame.'

'Are you really going to see that rascal's pig after the cheek he gave you?'

'Yes, of course. Stock up the car and let's be on our way.'

As we drove up the valley, I gave my student his first lesson on client psychology.

'There will be days when you wished you had never got out of bed, for in spite of what you do, things will go wrong and you will get blamed for it. But, happily, there are better days and these make it all worthwhile.

'Remember, young man, that he who kicks you one day may be your best friend later on. A similar incident happened to me a few months ago. Josiah Morris had a cow that was trying to calve; so he called in the local quack, Joe Phips. Now this character was all muscle and boasted he could lick any vet on pulling a calf. Joe worked on the poor heifer for over two hours and then gave up. I happened to be on call and answered their request for help.

'The wretched heifer was by this time stretched out on the straw. I saw the calf's head and part of one forelimb piled in the gutter, obviously having been removed by the local Tarzan! Her vagina was swollen and it was hard for me to work on her.

'Eventually, I managed to deliver the rest of the calf, gave the heifer some medicine and told the owner that things were not looking too good. I had hardly left the farm when the heifer died—which I had expected.'

'You see, Jim, the heifer already had a ruptured uterus before I went to work on her due to the reckless pulling by the lay operator. I learned a harsh lesson that afternoon and don't you ever forget it either.'

'What do you mean?'

'Well, I made the cardinal mistake of not letting the owner know her predicament as soon as I discovered her uterus was torn.'

'What difference does that make?'

'All the difference in the world. That old boy will never believe that I didn't do it!'

'So, Jim, my lad, always examine your patient well and be honest with your client.'

We reached Tim Harries's house, perched near a babbling brook at the end of the village. The surly, curly headed bachelor was waiting for us and led us to the pigsty with a low entrance. In the corner of the sty, almost hidden with straw was a massive Welsh sow. At the other corner was a bunch of anaemic looking piglets which made enough noise to wake the dead. But the old sow could not care less!

'The old stinker has the inflammation,' snorted our client. 'Give her something, quick!'

I pretended not to have heard him and proceeded to examine my patient. Her temperature was below normal and her ears were cold.

'She hasn't passed a thing since she farrowed yesterday.'

'That figures,' I muttered under my breath.

Jim had checked her udder and remarked that she had no milk. No wonder the little ones were squealing.

We went back to the car to get some medicine while the old man pulled on his crooked pipe, leaning against the wall.

'Jim, this is our chance to show this character a thing or two. Get me the P.O.P.'

'What's that?'

'Haven't you done any pharmacology yet?'

'Not much.'

'I need the posterior pituitary gland extract.'

'Is that a hormone?'

'Yes, come on or I'll catch it in the neck again!'

I placed a couple of cc's in a sterile syringe, cleaned the sow's right ear and injected the hormone slowly into the vein. Jim was crouched near the sow checking her breathing.

'Look, she is milking herself,' remarked my student in amazement.

Before he moved away, a stream of milk squirted into his eye!

'Fetch the piglets here and let them have their breakfast.'

Jim chased the little piglets in the straw and managed to get them to their mother. It was quite a sight seeing the twelve little devils nursing to their hearts' content.

'Will she get over it?' snarled old Tim, looking on with an air of disbelief.

'Of course. We'll give her some penicillin and you get her a warm bran mash.'

While Tim was getting the mash, Jim and I had a discussion in the pigsty.

'Why did you inject the hormone into the vein. Wouldn't it work just as well under the skin?' enquired my astute student.

'Yes, it would—but you see, Jim, this old boy didn't think we could do anything for his sow—except kill her. That's the kind of client who has to have the wonders of veterinary medicine demonstrated to him in 'shock waves'!'

'Well, that milk certainly caught me by surprise,' remarked Jim, with still a few milk spots on his cheek!

'Right! And you should have seen the old boy's expression. His pipe almost fell out of his mouth.'

'Well, we made a believer out of him in a hurry.'

The old sow snorted her thanks as we left the sty. Tim brought her the mash which she devoured heartily.

'Come in the house! I might as well pay you.' We sat at the kitchen table. The old man indeed must have been impressed.

Laugh and the whole world laughs with you. Weep—and you weep alone!

*   *   *

My busy practice meant that very often I would leave in the morning before our children got up and they would be in bed before I came home. This prompted Betsi, our little daughter, to remark to her mother on one of the rare days I was at home, 'Mam, my visiting father is here!'

As the children grew older, they loved coming out on calls with me. I used to drive rather fast and they shrieked with laughter as we sped over hump bridges on the country lanes. At the farms, they spent their time with the farmer's wife, eating biscuits, chocolates or some home baked pies, etc. Thomas was a work-horse and invariably got hold of the broom and swept the kitchen floor!

Our clients were very kind. Very often, I would arrive home with a chicken, home made pie, fish from the local river, or vegetables in season.

Sometimes I managed to get an evening free. On one occasion, as we were driving home, Thomas remarked, 'Mummy, the moon is following us.' Michael immediately chirped, 'Yes, and Jesus Christ is driving it!'

Whenever the practice was not so busy, I enjoyed attending the quarterly meetings of the South Wales Division, British Veterinary Association. It was a wonderful opportunity to meet my colleagues and exchange practice experiences over a cup of tea or other light refreshments after the meeting. I was President-Elect when I left for the United States and now an Honorary Life President.

Family time at Trevaughan, our new home in the mid 1950s; Dad, Michael, Thomas, Betsi and Mam. *Photo by W.D. Evans.*

Stick 'em up.

The Cat Lover

Ifor and I were having our usual scramble to gulp down our breakfast before scooting off on our bicycles to morning class—even nine o'clock was considered an unearthly hour for academic enrichment in our College days—when we overheard a loud conversation coming from the kitchen.

'Those terrible students were out so late last night I felt like locking them out!'

'Meow.'

'That's right, my love. You never go chasing those naughty girls, do you my sweet little bunch?'

'Grrrr-.'

Ifor almost choked on his toast and marmalade. There she goes again—our crazy landlady who almost had an obsession about cats. She was rather a lonely old spinster and probably life had not touched her. She rarely left her big three-storey house, full of antiques and all kinds of cats. There was Ben, a massive superbly masculine specimen of feline grandeur; Daniel, a scruffy looking black and white; Letticia, a cute little cat, but oh! what a scrapper; and Jemima, a three month old cuddly kitten as white as snow.

Ben was the subject of her conversation that morning. What caused Ifor and me such hysterics? Well, old Ben had been doctored recently. Sure, he didn't chase the 'girls' anymore, but we reckoned he still had a lot of pride and was probably a consultant to the rest of the 'he-men' in the neighbourhood.

Nellie Hills was a different kind of cat lover. Nellie loved her Siamese cats—all four of them. They were the resident family, but there were feline guests around also most of the time. Her husband was the landlord of the pub and like most of his kind, he could converse on any subject on earth. He was a handsome, middle-aged gentleman, and we spent many a late hour talking about our favourite sport of cricket. But my visits to the pub were to attend to one of the cats. Socializing and professional service don't always mix too well— especially when things go wrong!

I received a call from Nellie late one winter's evening. The landlord had called the customary 'Time, gentlemen, please', but there were still a few of the locals trying to get an extra pint for the road! The pubs closed officially at ten o'clock, but it was not unusual for the party to continue in the back kitchen. I was always sceptical about going to a pub through the back door lest I be accused of slipping in for a quick one! On a cold winter's night it wasn't really a bad idea and even the local Bobby enjoyed an occasional 'heart warmer'.

Nellie was really upset. Jimmy, her five year old Siamese tomcat had been missing all day and eventually hobbled in with a horrible looking cut on his left shoulder.

Mike, my third year student, was quite a ladies' man and especially liked cats. After our thorough examination for a foreign body in the wound and our relief to find no broken bones, we treated the case as an open wound which would probably heal better without suturing. We cleaned it as well as we could and dusted it with some antiseptic powder. An injection of antibiotics was also in order. Mike produced the necessary equipment and medication and proceeded to make the injection into a thigh muscle while Nellie held her precious pet close to her bosom. For some unknown reason our esteemed patient went berserk. He let out a horrible shriek and jumped all over the place. I have heard of cats on the rooftops and cats on the tiles, but this was quite a show—and a frightening one, too. Jimmy tore into the kitchen and across the table, knocking over several pints of bitter in his path. The locals took up the chase and finally got him into a corner of the pub. He hissed and clawed while poor Nellie went into hysterics. Why didn't we leave him alone? Well, the needle was still in his leg! Just as Mike thought he had Jimmy 'in the bag' by trying to wrap the landlord's heavy jacket over him, he bolted again all over the bar. 'It's an ill wind that blows nobody any good' and that's how it turned out here. Amid all the turmoil and turning her wrath on Mike and myself, it was quite a relief to both of us—when Nellie passed out on the pub floor! The local grocer and the butcher took care of her—probably with a face wash of cold beer.

Mike finally succeeded in capturing our elusive patient under the heavy jacket and removed the needle.

The phone rang. It was my wife with instructions about an urgent call far out in the country. Being called out late on a cold winter's night was almost to be expected. But were we glad to get away and our moonlight drive from the pub to Jack Rees's farm was devoted to a lengthy discussion about the psychology of cats and cat owners. My student proceeded with his usual attention to minutia to enlighten me. Apparently, according to my instructor, the Chinese believe that cat haters were re-incarnated rats!

A black cat in the British Isles is a sign of good luck, but not so in America. Many a loving mother has tucked away an emblem of a black cat and a threepenny piece in the pocket of her child before embarking out into the cold wide world.

'What about some of the history of cats in Wales?'

'An old Welsh King, *Hywel Dda* (Howell the Good) proclaimed a law which placed a price on cats. A new-born kitten was worth a penny and after it caught a mouse it fetched fourpence.'

'Do you really believe in these superstitions about cats? Can they foretell the weather?'

'Of course. If a cat turns its tail to the fire, there will be a hard frost; if it licks its tail, it will rain.'

'Can you tell anything by a cat's face?'

'Yes, the Chinese tell the time of day by the contraction and dilation of a cat's pupil.'

'I can tell a person's character by his eyes!'

'How do you do it?'

'There is no way I can tell you. It must be intuition or an inborn gift, but believe me, I can sum up a new client by the 'cut' of his eyes.'

'Mike, my boy, you may know a lot about cats, but I must warn you that they can get you off your high horse faster than lightning. Once there was a cocky veterinary student who thought he knew all about cats. He and the town's young doctor were close buddies and they agreed to spay a cat together. The medico had never seen one performed so he lined up his landlady's cat for the big occasion. Everything was set out meticulously, and the operation was soon in progress. The doctor was in charge of the anaesthesia. A perfect incision was made in the left flank and the search for the sex organs was initiated. There are times when it is hard to find the horns of the uterus in a fat cat.'

'The search continued, but to no avail; then, the moment of truth emerged! Was it really a she-cat? They reflected the surgical drape over the patient's hind limbs, and as clear as daylight, facing them were the most gorgeous pair of testicles imaginable!'

'This reinforces the importance of making a thorough examination of your patient, *always*. If most of us spent as much time examining the patient as we do in scrubbing up for a surgical operation, our professional competence would increase enormously.'

'Tis the Season to be Jolly

The stockings were full, and the last of our guests who came to our annual open house on Christmas Eve had left. Carlo, our Welsh Corgi, was neatly snuggled in his basket by the cooker in the kitchen, and it was time for Mary and me to retire for the night—or what was left of it since it was well past midnight. It had been an unusually hectic Christmas Eve.

Following a very busy schedule of calls all day, I found myself with the assignment of performing a surgical operation on a cow. That in itself was not uncommon. In fact, during the winter months we performed Caesarean operations on cows every week. But this one was different. The owner was also the landlord of a pub and an employee of the County Council, on the road crew. He was a short, thick-set old gentleman who was always neatly dressed in his corduroy trousers and flannel shirt and wore his cap flat on his head with the peak down over his forehead. Anna, his wife, was the publican by day. She was a generous soul who always looked on the bright side of life.

My patient was their well-fed pet Shorthorn cow which was tied in the little barn with a thatched roof, adjoining the pub. Word had spread around the pub that big things were happening in the barn. Some of the local characters had started their Christmas celebrations earlier in the day and were already 'three sheets to the wind.' They all wanted to help. Twm Hughes held the cow's tail in one hand and a pint of bitter in the other while 'Boxer' Price was delegated to keep the rest of the guests under control, seated on bales of straw at suitable vantage points. The operation was necessary because the calf was presented in the posterior or breach position with the hind limbs forward under the abdomen. Since the calf was also oversized, correcting the malpresentation would be difficult with the possibility of a ruptured uterus and maybe the loss of the calf.

Under local anaesthesia, the operation was performed in the standing position, in the lower left flank. Very soon a beautiful bull calf was delivered. My guests named him Noel. Lloyd was elated and beckoned to his wife to supply a round of Christmas cheer for everyone. Soon I was entertained with Christmas carols by my impromptu male voice choir! My patient started to chew her cud to her heart's content and Noel was soon standing and ready for his Christmas cheer from his mother.

Christmas Day that year was no exception. The children were swarming all over our bedroom displaying their gifts from Father Christmas long before Jack Thomas's cockerels down the road poured forth their song of praise to daybreak.

Someone had also forgotten to inform my patients that this was a special day to be spent with the family. Most of the years I was in practice, they seemed to get the message, but on this morning Dafydd Jenkins arrived with a lambing case. That in itself was unusual—at least a month early for the lambing season. However, I was grateful to him for bringing in my patient and for leaving his wife at home! I had a special affection for old Dafydd or *Dai Bach* as he was known in the neighbourhood. He was a short, slim little fellow who always wore his well-weathered cap backwards with the peak hanging down over the back of his neck. He walked with a stilting gait, and his right hand always perched on his right buttock. He was as honest as the day, but, bless his heart, he was probably the most hen-pecked little man in the country. His wife was a tall, pale faced, lanky-legged woman with a tongue like a whiplash. Her day was never right unless she had cursed old Dafydd a dozen times, or anyone else who crossed her path. She was known as 'Ferocious Annie', to her neighbours, but really her bark was worse than her bite. In fact, underneath this front there was a lot of kindness in the old girl. She always greeted me with several cuss words when I arrived at her farm at the edge of the village up the valley. At first, I was rather scared and my students were completely baffled by her 'reception'. I soon realized that the best defence was to look her in the face and smile. She invariably mellowed at this reaction.

Dafydd's ewe was a Shropshire which had brought triplets a year ago. This birth was obviously premature and on closer examination I noticed there were three small feet protruding from her vagina. The situation seemed to call for a Caesarean operation since the genitalia did not seem prepared for birth. However, being a Shropshire, she was a spacious ewe. To my surprise, I found that all three legs were the forelimbs of one lamb and with steady traction, I was able to deliver this freak, alive. Quite a Christmas present to take home for old Annie. She probably cursed the ram!

Dafydd and I retired to our warm kitchen and my Christmas Day was made by observing how he thoroughly enjoyed my wife's hospitality as he ate a sumptuous breakfast plus some Christmas cheer. He had quite an appetite for a little old man.

The rest of the day was a series of frustrations. First, there was a cow with milk fever about six miles up the valley. Just when I was getting ready to enjoy playing with the children's new toys which were still in one piece, another call came from the neighbouring farm to the one I had just visited. This cow had been sick for several days. This was about par for the course for this particular client who always expected a miracle.

My little Ford flew along that valley in great style and I was able to get home in time for our annual feast. Mary and our housemaid had excelled themselves again. Grandma Harries had joined us for the holidays, and she was a great favourite with all of us and the neighbours. Before getting down to the meal it was our custom to pull the crackers off with a bang, and inside each one there was a little gift and multicoloured paper hat to be worn during the Christmas dinner. There was plenty of turkey, sausage, bread sauce, mashed potatoes, mashed carrots and parsnips, and brussels sprouts. No matter how much we filled ourselves, there had to be room for the traditional Christmas pudding and brandy sauce. Mary would always hide threepenny pieces in the pudding and all of us anxiously dissected our slice of pudding in search of these elusive coins which were supposed to bring the finder lots of luck during the coming year.

*   *   *

I don't particularly dislike pigs. In fact, they are rather fascinating animals, but somehow, I always seemed to be called to a sick pig at the most unwelcome occasions such as Sunday afternoons, after a wedding, a funeral or a concert. Sure enough, my mid-Christmas afternoon nap was interrupted by a call to attend to an old sow with constipation. She belonged to Cora Pearce down on the Grist in Laugharne.

Cora was a cockle woman of Flemish origin. She greeted me with her usual stance—short, wide bosomed, with the usual black shawl, an old grey hat turned down at the brim, while her rolly polly, stubby legs bulged over her ankles, and she wore heavy wooden clogs. Her face was a picture to behold. Square jaws, tight lips, deep, slit-like blue eyes, and tough, leathery, heavily-wrinkled forehead and cheeks. When she smiled all that was left of her front teeth stuck out of the corners of her mouth like two miniature ivory tusks. Cora had seen hard times in her well-earned seventy five years. Her husband had spent most of his life sailing the high seas, and she was left to scratch a living for their six children. But she was a proud and tenacious old lady who knew every inch of the bay during her cockling expeditions. She was the cleaner woman at the local school and put in her shift at a local pub on weekends. Cora always raised a pig in her back yard which she tended with loving care.

Bertha, the old sow, was almost hidden in her straw bed and took no notice of my examination procedures. When I brushed back the straw, I could see that she was covered in diamond-shaped reddish blue plaques raised above the normal skin.

'Bertha has erysipelas.'

Cora put her hand to her right ear and remarked, 'Did you say my sow has the syphilis? Shame on you', was her muffled reply.

Cora was rather deaf and from under her shawl she produced a curved black trumpet-shaped contraption. She put one end to her ear and commanded me to communicate with her from the other end.

'No, Cora, I told you she had er-y-sip-el-as. You see those red bumps. That's what pig measles look like.'

'What did you say? Measles? My children had that years ago.'

'Alright, but that is different. No connection with children's measles.'

'Can you save her?'

'Yes, I believe I can. There is a new drug available now. I would like to try it. It's called penicillin.'

'Penny—what?'

'Pen-i-cil-lin.'

Bertha was a Welsh sow, a breed of pigs with lopped ears which cover most of the face. While Cora rubbed Bertha's belly, I slid a shot of the new wonder drug under the skin behind her ear.

'Now, we will have to do something about the constipation. I will need a quart of warm water and soap.'

'Are you going to drench her with that?'

'No, Cora, drenching might kill her. I never drench pigs. It's for the other end.'

Between us we gave Bertha the soap and water enema, and then Cora threw her hands up in the air and with her 'tusks' glowing in the gathering twilight, she hooted with laughter and remarked, 'Just what my old man needs once in a while!'

While I was getting cleaned up in the kitchen, Cora produced a bottle of her special elderberry wine and Christmas cake, complete with marzipan and icing. We had quite a party. Those cockle women were tough old girls with lots of character.

*   *   *

I am still not sure how Boxing Day derived its name. It certainly has nothing to do with fighting. There is one theory that boxes which were placed in churches for contributions were opened on this day. The tradition is apparently derived from an even older custom dating back to the Middle Ages. During that era, monks celebrated mass for the safety of ships, at the same time placing small boxes on each ship to receive contributions from the sailors.

Whatever its historical significance, Boxing Day in most parts of the country is a very special occasion as well as being a national holiday. It is *the* day of the year for fox hunting, but on many farms, groups of neighbours spend the time ferreting. A ferret is a half-tamed albino variety of the polecat. They are often rather vicious little animals which are kept muzzled most of the time because of their rasping teeth. When I was in Standard One in school there was quite a sensation when Ianto Tŷ Draw brought one to school. Ianto was quite a hero—until the little rascal ran loose, all over the classroom. Did he not have a hot back side after the Headmaster was through with him!

Ferreting was a very popular sport in my youth. As soon as the barns were cleaned and the milking buckets washed, away we would go to the neighbour's farm where old Jim had supposedly the best ferret in the parish. He also had in Queenie the skinniest whippet I have ever known. Whippets are miniature greyhounds—and whew, how they can run!

This particular Boxing Day, we took off from Jim's farmyard full of anticipation that this was going to be quite a show. In accordance with the custom in ferreting, Queenie was taken out of the canvass sack in which she was carried around, and pushed down a rabbit hole in one of the hedges. In a matter of seconds, out bolted three rabbits. Like a flash of lightning, Jim's whippet tore after them and soon had his first catch of the day. Jim was a proud old man whose ginger moustache always seemed to bristle when things were going right. He was, nevertheless, a boastful chap who claimed that *his* ferret would always do what he wanted—but alas this was not his day.

All went well for a couple of hours. Rabbits were bolting out of their holes all along the hedgerow until suddenly, nothing happened— well, not exactly. When he put Queenie into another hole, the rabbits came out but there was no sign of Queenie. The little shyster had decided to 'lodge'. Whenever you go ferreting, you are always afraid this will happen as for some reason, the ferret sometimes decides to stay underground.

Well, there was nothing to do but collect some straw, stuff it into the hole and put a match to it. This august ceremony is known as 'smoking out the ferret.' In most cases it worked—the ferret comes out from a connecting hole. But poor Jim, he was aghast. Queenie didn't budge. Needless to say, we, the neighbourhood children were highly amused—Jim's Queenie doing this!

It was just like Delme Hughes to burst out laughing in front of him. He was banished to the farmyard to fetch a couple of shovels and a pick axe. There was nothing else to be done—we would have to dig Queenie out—which we managed to do before sunset.

Bon Voyage! Gathering of clients, friends and relatives at Gwalia Hall, St. Clears.
Photos by W. D. Stroud, Laugharne.

Go West Young Man

'Go west young man
To the land of the free
Where the mighty Missouri
runs down to the sea'

There was nothing unusual about that Saturday morning in May, 1961. Ron, my student and I had tuberculin tested several herds and vaccinated a bunch of calves against brucellosis (Bang's disease). We returned rather late for a lunch of fish and chips which was our usual menu on Saturdays. Mary brought in the mail and I noticed there was a letter from overseas. It was an invitation from Dr. J. Wiley Wolfe, Head of the Department of Medicine and Surgery, Oklahoma State University. He offered me the position of Instructor in the Large Animal Section with a salary of 7,200 dollars plus fringe benefits. When I read it out, the children expressed their immediate approval that I should accept it, adding 'now we can see *real* Cowboys and Indians.' Mary chuckled for she knew only too well how deeply entrenched I was in our practice and all of us in the community life.

A couple of weeks rolled by, and eventually, I wrote for more information.

To the consternation of our families, friends, and clients, Mary and I decided to 'cross the Rubicon'—and head West.

We sold our home and the furniture. We packed our clothes and personal items for shipment overseas. Our clients and friends came to Gwalia Hall in the village and gave us a most memorable send-off, with gifts, several speeches of gratitude and best wishes. We will never forget the singing, especially the national anthem of Wales, *Hen Wlad Fy Nhadau*.

On Thursday, October 23, 1961, we left Southampton, England, aboard the *Queen Elizabeth* for a new life in the United States on the plains of Oklahoma. As we sailed along the English Channel, I could see the Welsh coastline and recalled the wonderful singing at the Village Hall:

We'll keep a welcome in the hillsides
We'll keep a welcome in the vales.
This land you knew will still be singing
When you come home again to Wales.
This land of song will keep a welcome
With a love that never fades.
We'll kiss away each hour of hiraeth
When you come home again to Wales.

Leaving Southampton.

Postscript

The *Queen Elizabeth* docked at New York harbour on Halloween Day, October 31, 1961 after a five-day voyage with almost everyone seasick on the second day.

The Williams family took a train from Grand Central Station overnight to Chicago. The following evening they rode the Texas Chief to Perry, Oklahoma, arriving at 7:00 the following morning. They were met in the rain by Dr. E. Wynn Jones, who drove them to his home in Stillwater where they stayed with him, his wife, Sam, and newly arrived daughter, Sarah, until they bought a home, complete with the furniture, three weeks later.

The children enrolled in the local schools. Thomas and Michael had crew cuts and long pants, to be in line with the other students. Thomas was elected President of the Student Council for his senior year at High School and lettered in football and track. He was also chosen to go to Boys State. Michael lettered in wrestling and sang in the school choirs. The boys also reached the rank of Eagle Scouts. Betsi was active in several organizations including Student Council and Girl Scouts.

The family joined the First Presbyterian Church. Eric and Mary were elected Elders. After the mandatory five year residency requirements, they became citizens of the United States.

Thomas received a degree in Business Administration from Oklahoma State University (OSU) where he was a member of Delta Tau Delta Fraternity and the Student Union Activities Board. After graduation he worked for a year as Chapter consultant for his Fraternity. He is currently the Executive Director of Stillwater YMCA, an Elder at the First Presbyterian Church, and a member of the Kiwanis Club having served as Lieutenant Governor. He had the honour of being selected to the team to carry the Olympic Torch when it came through Stillwater on Sunday, May 19, 1996, on its way to the Olympics in Atlanta, Georgia. Thomas and his wife, Emily, have a son, Bryn, aged 4.

Michael attended OSU for a year and then enlisted in the United

States Air Force. He became involved in air-sea rescue missions. Later he served a tour of duty in Viet Nam as a Loadmaster on a C-130 transport plane with the 345th Tactical Airlift Squadron. He received the Distinguished Flying Cross and three Air Medals. After discharge from the USAF, Michael pursued a career in hotel and restaurant management. He is presently employed as Marketing Director for the Ironwood Country Club in Palm Desert, California. Michael and his wife, Kathleen, have a son, Dylan, aged 7 and a daughter, Ariana, aged 5.

Betsi received a degree in Speech Communication Consultancy at OSU where she was a member of Kappa Delta Sorority and active in intra-mural functions. She was a leader in church youth society. Betsi is presently a business manager in Tulsa where she lives with her husband, Perry, daughter, Sarah, aged 16, and Mark, aged 12. The family is active in the First Christian Church, with Perry and Betsi serving as deacons and the children leaders in the youth groups.

Mary is a homemaker and continues to be active in the community. She has sung in the First Presbyterian Church Choir for over 30 years. When the Mobile Meals program was started in 1972, Mary was a member of the original team and has delivered meals weekly ever since. She has contributed over 10,000 hours of volunteer service at the Stillwater Medical Center, mainly in the Gift Shop and received the Altrusa Service Award in 1982. Mary is a member of P.E.O.

Eric taught courses in large animal medicine and surgery at the College of Veterinary Medicine for many years and reached the rank of Professor. He specialized in cattle internal medicine and received the Master of Science degree in Veterinary Pathology at OSU. He is a Charter member of the American College of Veterinary Internal Medicine. In later years he also became the college Director of Student and Alumni Affairs. He was the host of the TV series 'Oklahoma Vet'. He served as Chairman of the OSU Faculty Council (highest elected office) in 1971-72 and also on the OSU Athletic Council. He is the recipient of college and university teaching awards. Other recognitions include the Oklahoma Vet of the Year Award in 1980 (first recipient), AVMA International Award, 1981 and the RCVS Clinical Medal in 1994. He served as Editor, *The Oklahoma Vet* for 25 years and is currently the Editor of *The Bovine Practitioner* and the *Proceedings* for the American Association of Bovine Practitioners (AABP) having served for 26 years. In 1985, the AABP established the Amstutz-Williams Award in honour of Dr. Harold Amstutz, long-time Executive Secretary and the Editor who were the first recipients. Eric served on the Board of Trustees, Stillwater Medical Center (SMC) for 12 years, including 2 years as Chairman and on the Board of Directors of SMC Foundation. He is a member of Stillwater Lions Club. He wrote the histories of the OSU College of Veterinary Medicine, First Presbyterian Church and Stillwater Medical Center.

The Eric and Mary Williams Endowment Fund was established at the Oklahoma State University Foundation in 1992. Part of the proceeds from the sale of these books will be donated to the Fund

The Eric and Mary Williams Endowment Fund

The Eric and Mary Williams Endowment Fund was established in 1992 at the Oklahoma State University Foundation with contributions from colleagues and friends following Dr. Williams' retirement. A substantial donation was also received from the American Association of Bovine Practitioners.

The Fund may be used for any of the following:

The student delegate from the OSU College of Veterinary Medicine to attend the annual Congress of the International Veterinary Students Association.

A stipend for a veterinary medical graduate student from a third world country to study food animal medicine, with emphasis on herd health and nutrition programmes, at the OSU College of Veterinary Medicine.

A stipend for a vet to carry out an assignment in food animal medicine, focused on herd health and nutrition programmes, in a third world country.

Party time on board the *Queen Elizabeth*.